GUIDING

HOW TO ARTFULLY INSPIRE, INFLUENCE, AND DRIVE LASTING *change*

CHANGE

CHRISTIE COOPER PHD

Guiding Change
How to Artfully Inspire, Influence, and Drive Lasting Change
Christie Cooper © 2025

Hardcover ISBN: 978-1-61206-368-3
Softcover ISBN: 978-1-61206-369-0

For more information, visit CooperConsultingGroup.com

To purchase this book at quantity discounts, contact Aloha Publishing at alohapublishing@gmail.com

Published by

AlohaPublishing.com

Printed in the United States

To all those who need to
be inspired to change.

Contents

Introduction

> " Progress is impossible without change, and those who cannot change their minds cannot change anything. "
>
> —George Bernard Shaw

The last century has brought with it rapid changes unlike anything people throughout history have experienced before, and the speed with which the world changes only seems to increase each year. Change is an inherent part of life, and how individuals handle it is vital to their workplace roles.

When organizational change is inevitable, an individual's relevance in the workplace relies upon their ability to handle change. Strong change management skills can help even individuals who struggle with change to adapt more easily while promoting the success of the organization as a whole.

Organizations go through change for a wide variety of reasons, such as downsizing and restructuring due to rising costs or lack of revenue, to remove underperforming employees, to eliminate unneeded management, or simply to increase efficiency. One of the most common structural changes happening now is for organizations to shift into flatter, leaner forms of leadership rather than relying on the more traditional, hierarchical management structures.

Perhaps more than anything else, advances in technology have shaped the organizational landscape and increased the speed of change.

With more than 25,000 mergers and acquisitions in the U.S. in 2021 alone (Statista, 2024), it's clear that organizational change is common. According to Deloitte, between 2020 and 2024, over 80,000 mergers and acquisitions were reported, which was a dramatic increase from many previous years.

The need to change in order to remain relevant and competitive is an inherent part of today's business world, and it brings with it potential for many positive developments, such as improved profits, enhanced efficiency, and better employee engagement.

However, managing change comes with a host of challenges. When companies aren't properly prepared for change, the process quickly becomes messy and creates disruption, confusion, and chaos within the workplace. On an individual level, it can create anxiety, anger, or resistance. When people perceive something as going wrong, it's difficult for them to focus on anything else, and it can create a defensive attitude.

Unfortunately, poor change management is often the norm within the U.S. Recently a major leadership development company experienced some layoffs. You'd think such a company would

> **"There is nothing permanent except change."**
>
> —Heraclitus

be good at managing change because they coach their clients through such issues, but the layoffs were handled quite poorly. Employees were asked to accept the change and get on board or leave.

I spoke to a team member who worked for this company. He was called and told that he would be laid off, and within five minutes, his computer completely shut down. A handful of other people received the same treatment. This could have been handled with much more sensitivity. For example, they could have had a Zoom meeting for everyone who was laid off to honor their contributions and give the remaining employees the opportunity to say what they appreciated about those people. It would have given people the chance to process and those who were leaving to do so on a better note, feeling the sincere appreciation of their team. But they didn't give anyone that opportunity.

When companies are focused on the end result of change rather than on the process, that change may often fail. They want people to jump to the destination without thinking of the psychological effect the change will have on their team members.

In the case of layoffs or reorganizations, many of the employees who remain with the company have to deal with survivor guilt. They may grieve the loss of their coworkers who may have been close friends. People begin to feel less secure in their own jobs after such changes, leading to disengagement and sometimes additional turnover.

In many cases, poor change management can lead to defensiveness, which often becomes resistance to change. People may feel the change is unnecessary, that things were working just fine previously. Organizational change managed poorly leads to trust erosion among individuals and teams.

Change isn't always a negative occurrence. It's when change is imposed on people that they're more likely to become resistant. Whether the change is accepted or rejected is very situational, depending on their perspective and how it affects them. Managers need to understand that people react to change differently. An important influencing factor in how people react is their behavioral style. Those who are more risk-activated and prefer to take things at a faster pace may be excited by change, while those who are more risk-inhibited generally tend to react with more trepidation.

Excellent change management requires leaders to understand how people psychologically process change and then use that knowledge to help people adapt. Understanding the personalities of your team members as individuals allows you insight into their reactions to change and how they process it.

This individualized, behavioral style-based approach has been missing from the research and conversation around change management for quite some time. I set out to close that gap with my research on attitudes toward organizational change, which was based on the DISC behavioral style model. Through that research, I discovered notable differences in attitudes toward organizational change between different DISC behavioral styles, which I've found to be a useful understanding for managing change. It allows leaders to understand where their people are coming from and address each person where they are.

I spent a significant portion of my career working for a major family-owned business in pet food sales. Every 18-24 months, the company underwent organizational shifts they called a "revitalization." Trust me, there was nothing revitalizing about it.

During a revitalization, every employee was evaluated to determine their job status in the future. So you might be living and working in California and told you were being offered a new position in Oklahoma—if you didn't like it, you could exit the business with a severance package of two weeks for every year you'd worked for the company. It could happen to anybody, even if you were the highest-performing team member.

Part of the point of these revitalizations was trying to find new efficiencies and was often dictated by the creation of new territories, new business mergers, or increasing the number of direct reports for managers—generally growing while making operations run leaner.

This kind of reorganization is not uncommon in large companies. One coaching client I had works for a very large medical and dental distributor, and she had to re-interview for her job and went from managing a team of 14 people to 65. Obviously, a change like that is overwhelming.

Through all of the revitalizations I experienced, I started to feel a little on edge, like many of my coworkers did. We saw our coworkers get laid off and moved around frequently and knew it may eventually happen to our own roles. It fostered a lot of uncertainty and eroded trust and made some people search for other jobs.

In my late 20s, I began working for a privately held pet food company, and after seven years, one of the largest family-owned

" There is nothing so stable as **change**. "

—Bob Dylan

organizations in the U.S. bought the company. I was excited about it because I knew this company put a lot of emphasis on learning and development and were a highly diverse organization, where I'd previously been the only woman out of a group of around 40 managers. I was ready to innovate and grow in my career. My optimistic attitude held up for a few years, but after I'd experienced my first few revitalizations, I realized that many of the people who'd been on my team were no longer working for the company—they had gone to work for competitors, and I wasn't allowed to talk business with my former colleagues any longer. That loss of camaraderie hit me pretty hard.

I stayed with the company and was determined to do the very best job I could because doing so made me feel good as an individual. But I knew that my path in the future would look different. I wanted to have more control over my future rather than getting moved around by the corporation.

A position opened up for VP of sales, so I put my name in the hat for it. And at the same time, I applied for Pepperdine's doctoral program for organizational leadership. I figured one of those doors would be opened, and whichever door opened was the one that I was going to step through.

Well, I didn't get the VP of sales job. In fact, they hired someone I felt was unqualified for the position, who would then be my boss. After sulking for about a week, I decided I'd do everything I could to make his life as easy as possible because I knew there were others around me who felt the same way I did. If I could help him be successful, my team would be successful, and it would be a win-win for everybody, especially the organization.

Eventually, my new boss did some things that I felt crossed an ethical line, so I decided then that in the future I would start my own business and blaze my own path. At the time, I was going to Pepperdine and working on my doctorate degree while I was still working. It was a difficult balance. One year I attended a national sales meeting and left slightly early to get on a plane to fly to Orange County to make it to my class on Tuesday night. Then I took a red-eye back home to be ready for the meeting the next day. I didn't want people to see my going back to school as something that would interfere with my job.

My goal was to open up my own company in the future, so on my vacation time, I conducted training workshops for clients outside of my industry just to practice my craft. By the time the next revitalization arrived, I was at peace with the prospect of being laid off. I knew it would provide me the impetus to pursue my long-term goal of starting my own company.

"In any given moment, we have two options: to step **forward** into growth or step **back** into safety."

—Abraham Maslow

1

Why Is Change Management Important?

At some point, every organization must face change, and as the rate of change only gets faster, companies that wish to thrive must prioritize change management. Those that don't invite chaos either by implementing change poorly or by failing to stay adaptable and competitive.

Too many businesses fail to adapt because they're comfortable with how things are. When things seem to be working well, business leaders may fail to question processes and challenge the way things are done.

Comfortable is not a good place to be.
Comfort creates blinders to what's going on around you.

Getting complacent can be a death sentence. As a consultant to companies managing change, the last words I want to hear are "This is how we've always done things around here."

Companies that fail to innovate or change to keep up with industry advancements inevitably fail, even brands that once seemed indestructible. When you look back to the turn of the century, it's easy to identify several iconic companies that suffered that very fate, such as Kodak or Blackberry. Blackberry devices were

"Change before you have to."

—Jack Welch

once a primary mode of communication for many people, but the popularity of iPhones and other mobile phones quickly made them obsolete. Blackberry didn't innovate quickly enough to keep up with the rapidly developing industry.

Similarly, Kodak and Polaroid were both camera brands that once dominated their markets but failed to adapt with the rise of digital cameras and eventually phone cameras. While both of these brands still exist today, they are primarily novelty products for hobbyists rather than the industry leaders they once were.

The difference between a company that innovates and one that resists change was also illustrated by the battle between Netflix and Redbox, both companies that offered DVD rentals; it's clear which one remained relevant as a result of adapting their business model with changing technology.

Companies like these demonstrate the need for businesses to remain agile and adaptable, which requires strong change management. Poor change management can be as damaging as resistance to change because it often leads to failed change. It's commonly said that 50-70 percent of change initiatives fail. It is about time to change that statistic!

Strong change management begins with leaders making sound decisions about when change is necessary or advantageous. It's also possible to be too driven toward change or to move too quickly, which can lead to risky or unnecessary changes that cause unneeded disruption to workflow or may move the organization in an unfavorable direction.

As a leader, you need to balance comfort and risk by remaining constantly prepared for change without jumping hastily into it. Understand and evaluate the developments needed to stay up-to-date with what's going on in your field and make changes with purpose. Evaluate processes regularly to determine what is and isn't working.

Sometimes what's needed is to simply take your company's employee manual or standard operating procedure, go through each item, and ask whether it's still needed and relevant. Sometimes the answer is yes, so it's always worthwhile to consult the people most closely involved in the work to understand the purpose of any procedure. But sometimes the answer is that a system is outdated and change is needed.

You can question and challenge the way things are done without leaping forward into change. Behavioral styles that are more risk-activated may jump into change too quickly, while risk-averse personalities may be too hesitant to change. But every style has something to contribute, so it can be beneficial to listen to different voices to understand the matter from a variety of perspectives.

"Change is the law of life. And those who look only to the past or present are certain to miss the future."

—John F. Kennedy

" The secret of **change** is to focus all of your energy not on fighting the old, but on building the **new**. "

—Socrates

2

Why Does Change Fail?

The culture at my former employer was to shake things up every couple years or so with "revitalizations." The first time I experienced one of these, it came as a shock. No one told me it was coming. It wasn't in the employee manual. But every 18-24 months, there would be some kind of reorganization.

As a manager, one of the steps I went through with each revitalization was a process where all the managers met to give feedback about everyone we knew. The company had forms for us to fill out, and I had to give feedback about everyone on my team, as well as anyone else I'd worked with in the organization. The forms were tallied up and the feedback was used to determine who would and would not be given offers to continue their jobs.

It baffled me that someone who did a really good job might be cut, and sometimes the people who were doing a poor job were kept.

Relocations were also common. Someone on my team in California was told to relocate to Oklahoma if he wanted to keep his job. The person was a surfer, yet he picked up his wife and three kids and moved from California to the middle of Tornado Alley. He stayed there for two years, until a spot opened back up on my team and I could hire someone. I asked if we could bring him back to California because he was an excellent team member. So the company paid to relocate him back to California.

The revitalizations created a reorganization culture with a lot of fear in the workforce.

People were worried that they'd lose their jobs, and rightfully so. I remember many people couldn't sleep, weren't eating, or were generally irritable or depressed. Some people adopted an attitude that there was nothing they could do about it and chose not to worry, but I bet even those people talked to their spouses about it because it impacted everyone. And each person's family was affected by it too.

Eventually, each person met one-on-one with HR. If you met with just your manager, you were safe. But if you met with your manager and HR, it meant you were getting a severance package.

Whether you were rehired or not, you had to sign a release form saying you wouldn't disclose any information you'd learned that day or you could lose your job. Everything was kept under wraps.

" The greatest danger in times of turbulence is not the turbulence— it is to act with yesterday's logic. "

—Peter Drucker

All of that change led to a lack of trust by the employees. After going through several revitalizations, you knew that at some point, your time might come to be cut. That worry erodes trust, and it makes it difficult for people to give their all to the job.

That's made even more difficult when the change results in making workers' jobs more difficult through cuts to resources. Often, the headcount gets lowered and people are asked to do more things for the same salary or in a smaller amount of time. That can be irritating or even defeating, and it often leads to disengagement.

When change fails, it doesn't necessarily mean the change isn't implemented. Failure can also include negative outcomes as a result of poor change management. It could also look like a process that takes longer to implement than necessary because of confusion among stakeholders. It might mean missed deadlines, higher costs that exceed budget, and issues for customers or clients as a result of the change.

In some cases, failed change can mean that the organization reverts back to the status quo it had before the change with the intent to regroup, and from there they might reintroduce the same change or modify the plan. Other times, they might completely abandon the change.

One of my clients, a multibillion-dollar company, created a new software system that connected everything in the company and distributed information across the organization. It was used for planning, purchasing, procurement, inventory management, sales, and marketing, among other things. This organization had a new leader who had been with the company for maybe about six months before the new software initiative began, and it was her first big project where she could showcase her skill set.

She wanted to ensure that her direct reports would be responsible for managing important aspects of the implementation. However, she didn't monitor the change or communicate with the team very well, and it left the team feeling disconnected. She simply expected her team to communicate all of the aspects of the change to everyone else in the organization.

Her lack of change management led to major problems with the implementation that caused it to take much longer than expected and lost the company a significant amount of money. If she'd made an effort to communicate the change and monitor its execution across departments, she could have prevented those losses.

CHALLENGES TO ORGANIZATIONAL CHANGE

It's common to run into challenges throughout the process of organizational change, many of which can lead to failure, delay, or costly chaos. What follows are a few of the most common issues organizations experience.

EMPLOYEE RESISTANCE

When a change is unpopular with employees, resistance can slow or even halt a change altogether. In many cases, team members need to be committed for a change to be effective, and even in instances where buy-in isn't necessary for the change to take place, resistance and negative feelings can cause a variety of other issues within the organization. While leaders may believe their employees' reactions are outside of their control, there are many ways that employee acceptance and buy-in can be facilitated through change management.

POOR COMMUNICATION

Perhaps the most common problem that hinders change initiatives is a lack of proper communication about the change. It's always best to over-communicate so that everyone understands what is happening, why it is needed, and what their role in the initiative looks like. Confusion leads to chaos, so it's up to leaders to communicate effectively and check in with groups and individuals to ensure understanding.

LACK OF RESOURCES

Making changes is expensive, and it can be difficult to see the costs associated with a planned change from the beginning. It's common to underestimate the resources needed to implement a change, which can cause the initiative to be delayed or even fail.

Leaders should carefully assess not only the expected costs but also other potential expenses that could arise and factor them into the budget.

POOR PLANNING

Sometimes organizations jump into a change without a strong plan for implementation and management, which can create a chaotic environment and lead to confusion and more employee resistance.

Strong change management requires leaders to account for possible challenges they'll encounter in implementing the change and prepare for them.

One of the biggest stories in the history of golf was announced on June 6, 2023—a merger between Saudi-backed LIV Golf and the U.S. PGA Tour. The framework agreement was made after many weeks of secret negotiations.

Jay Monahan, PGA (Pro Golfers Association) Tour Commissioner, along with Yasir Al-Rumayyan, Governor of the Saudi Arabia Public Investment Fund, announced in an interview that they wanted to unify the game of golf. Monahan shared on *Squawk on the Street*, "We can have a far greater impact on this game than we can working apart." In the Netflix Series *Full Swing*, PGA tour players Justin Thomas and Collin Morikawa shared their shock at the news. Many of the pro players found out through a Twitter announcement about the merger. Shockwaves traveled through the golf community. Trust had been eroded by the two sides of golf.

A backstory might be needed for non-golf players. The PGA was the eminent organization pro golfers played for. Then a new entity emerged: LIV Golf, a group funded by the Saudi Public Investment Firm. LIV Golf lured PGA players like Phil Mickelson and Dustin Johnson by offering huge monetary incentives to play for them. It was rumored that many big PGA players were offered nine figure sign-on bonuses to come play for LIV. This prompted the PGA to ban any LIV golfer from playing in PGA-sanctioned events. And here the rift began.

So in 2023, senior leaders in the PGA had a planning meeting to discuss the best way to announce the merger to their players at an event in Canada. Monahan met with all the players to answer questions. Even though the PGA is a player-backed organization, no one from the PGA consulted with the players about the merger prior to the merger announcement. The players were in the dark just like the public.

PGA tour player Rory McIlroy, a marquee player who was courted by LIV Golf for tremendous sums but remained loyal to the PGA, shared his shock and disbelief on *Full Swing*: "Being blindsided created much anger among the players and the announcement could have been handled much better." Rory went on in his interview to say, "You've galvanized everyone against something, and that thing you've galvanized everyone against, you've now partnered with . . . It is a hard pill to swallow."

This sports merger made big news. As of March 2025, the reunification of the two golf clubs had still not happened and talks were underway. Mergers are some of the largest changes organizations face and can be fraught with difficulty. Everyone who has to undergo change is affected by the stages of evolution, which we will discuss in chapter 6. This pro golf example is one demonstration of the first stage in change or evolution: acknowledgment. Change management is often the determining factor in whether those involved resist the change or accept and embrace it, helping to push the initiative toward success.

"Don't be afraid to give up the good to go for the great."

—John D. Rockefeller

3

What Makes Change Difficult?

One of the most common—and most disastrous—mistakes I see leaders make in managing change is underestimating the human element. They simply announce a change and expect everyone to buy into it with little time or assistance to process. And while some individuals may quickly adapt and take the change in stride, others inevitably struggle, leading to resistance, depression, and interruptions in workflow, among other problems.

Adapting to change is a skill set, and some people are more skilled at adapting than others.

Those who are better at adapting to change have developed the cognitive and emotional tools to handle it, such as open-mindedness, flexibility, and empathy.

One example of poor change management came from a major U.S. distribution company where one of the senior leaders announced that the job of her direct report, who was a manager, would be eliminated. This was on a group call in front of about 50 people, including that manager and her direct reports. Hearing that her job was being eliminated at the same time as everyone else did put her in a difficult position, as she tried to keep her composure throughout the meeting. Not to mention the shock felt by the rest of the team, who were surprised since she was such an excellent manager. When the call ended, the manager received an influx of calls from her direct reports who were all upset with the company, wondering how they could do this to her.

This manager's boss knew about the change ahead of time, and at the very least could have taken the time to notify her so she could prepare herself.

For the manager's team, a message like that can create insecurity. They may wonder if the same thing could happen to them, causing them to become disengaged and begin looking for other jobs because they don't want to be on the chopping block next. They might vent to other coworkers and spend time not getting work done because they're preoccupied with what's just happened. They'll have to adjust to the new leadership structure, and overall, it creates a large interruption in their workflow.

Organizational change has a major impact on everyone involved. It often requires people to make big adjustments like these:

- Changing workflow processes

- Taking on new responsibilities

- Working under new leadership or with new team members

- Experiencing differences in payment structure or benefits

Major changes like these affect their professional and their personal lives. If you're an employee whose organization is undergoing a major change, you may lose valued colleagues you respected, which can lead to survivor guilt, trust erosion, and feelings of uncertainty. Frequent changes can cause worries about when the next major change will happen.

Inevitably, change causes interruption in workflow and routines, which are difficult adjustments for many people.

Leaders can also struggle with organization change, both from a personal perspective and through the lens of change management. Workflow interruptions can affect the quality of customer or client service, which may affect the company's bottom line. Leaders need to develop skill sets for adapting as well as managing change, including empathy, influence, and the ability to ask for and listen to feedback. They need communication skills to articulate the change in a way that's relatable and understandable. That requires storytelling to paint the vision for the future, the steps to get there, and how each person's role contributes to the new vision.

In addition, leaders need to manage resistance, which happens primarily through one-on-one conversations. Leaders may encounter frustration when team members struggle to commit to the change, and it can be challenging to determine when someone resistant to change needs to be let go. Leaders should give everyone the space and opportunity to adapt, but there comes a point when someone is a hindrance to the change or the organization because of their resistance.

I worked with a company that made a change to their payroll process. My company delivered monthly sessions to their leaders as part of a year-long leadership program. However, by the end of that year, a small faction of the team were still disgruntled about their new payroll system and made it known. At some point, the change has to happen, and each person will have to reckon with that. Some individuals will get on board and others will actively disengage. Those who are actively disengaged or resistant can become toxic to the organization.

There's a saying among managers that you hire for skill and fire for attitude. If leaders have given people time to adjust and have helped people work through the psychological process of adapting to change and are still receiving resistance, they need to evaluate whether those individuals should still be part of the organization.

The most difficult part of organizational change is managing the emotional responses of the stakeholders, those affected by the change. There are several categories of responses to change that leaders need to consider and plan for when they are managing change:

- Emotional responses

- Interruptions to business as usual

- Survivor guilt

- Trust and security issues

- "We feeling"

- Change fatigue

- Resistance to change

All of these responses are possible and can hinder a successful change. Let's look at them in more depth so they are easier to recognize and mitigate.

EMOTIONAL RESPONSES

Leaders may overlook the emotional responses of their team members, but those responses are an important part of processing the change. Leaders need to be in tune with what's going on with their team members. Leaders may feel frustration in getting team members on board. What may seem simple to a leader isn't necessarily as simple for team members to wrap their heads around.

Action Tip: Understanding how individuals respond to change and checking in with them regularly can help leaders get a better picture of how someone is processing change and what kind of support they may need to get on board. Personality plays an influential role in responses to change, so leaders need a strong understanding of their own personality as well as the personalities and behavioral styles of their team members.

This can be difficult when the leader feels they have a lot going on that they need to manage. However, some elements of change management can be delegated to others, which helps those individuals become a part of the process to create better buy-in.

INTERRUPTIONS

Change of any kind almost always creates an interruption. Even if the change doesn't dramatically affect processes (and most changes do affect processes to some extent), employees still have to deal with their psychological and emotional reactions, which create an interruption to their workflow. Interruptions affect the organization at every level, from individuals to teams and even the company's revenue, as it impacts productivity and quality of service.

When organizations go through mergers, there's often a duplication of positions, which means someone is excused from their role. If the person who now performs that role isn't happy and leaves, the organization can end up with a position that needs to be filled anyway. It can be time-consuming and expensive to try to find the right people.

Organizations also need to consider how change may affect their customers or clients. I knew a pharmaceutical company that created a new ERP (enterprise resource planning) system that affected how their vendors and partners got paid. There was so much internal turmoil over the change process that it affected the way they treated their customers.

Excellent change management is needed to prevent these kinds of interruptions that can be detrimental to the organization as a whole.

Dealing with the complications of interruptions to productivity can make emotionally processing the change even more challenging and complicates change management.

Action Tip: Account for additional time to see the change through due to interruptions. People who are resistant or blockers to change may slow down the process. Be sure to bring everyone along. Communication is key during a change.

SURVIVOR GUILT

If colleagues are eliminated in the change, those who are left behind may develop survivor guilt. It's a very similar type of psychological stress to what happens when a few people survive a big accident where others are killed. Those who remain may feel happy or grateful to still have their jobs, but they often also feel guilty because they recognize that those who were eliminated also have families and bills to pay.

Action Tip: Offer internal support such as coaching and mentorship to help individuals feel valued and understand their role within the company and its future. Additionally, outplacement services can be provided to those team members who are exiting the business.

TRUST AND SECURITY

Major changes or frequent changes can erode employees' trust in the company as people begin to worry about what might happen next. In the case of roles being eliminated, people might wonder if they'll be the next ones to be eliminated. Eliminating roles often results in further frustration as employees are frequently asked to take on new or additional responsibilities, sometimes having to do more work with fewer resources for the same pay. In some cases, they may lose faith that the organization has their best interests in mind. This kind of trust erosion can cause people to check out from their roles, doing the bare minimum required while still taking a paycheck. Others may begin to look for other employment opportunities because they're dissatisfied or worried about being eliminated.

I've seen companies lose top-performing employees after large changes or layoffs. And an employee who leaves to work for a competitor may take some of your company's client base with them because those clients like working with that individual. So not only do you lose a high-performing employee, but you can also lose top clients.

Action Tip: As a leader, proactively consider potential clients that might be lost due to the elimination of employees. Visit with those customers to build rapport and work to keep their business.

"WE FEELING"

The term "we feeling" refers to the collective emotional response of employees undergoing significant changes. That emotional response is often a mix of feelings depending on the nature of the change and the perspectives of the individual involved, but it can include anxiety, fear, uncertainty, excitement, hope, frustration, or resistance. These feelings often shape the atmosphere of the environment and can spread among team members. If a few team members have a highly negative response to the change, there's a risk that resistance can spread through "we feeling," creating greater resistance.

Action Tip: Check in with teams and individuals regularly to keep an eye on the collective atmosphere and attitude. While a few negative individuals can poison the well, "we feeling" can also be influenced in a positive direction by champions of change.

CHANGE FATIGUE

Change fatigue tends to occur when changes are frequent or extended over a long period of time. Dealing with change can be quite difficult and draining, so pacing of change is an important factor in its success, since change fatigue may result in resistance.

According to Prosci's model of change, symptoms of change fatigue that leaders should watch out for include the following (Kempton, 2021):

- Noise – More frequent and louder complaints about changes

- Apathy – Growing indifference about project changes, with some completely disengaging; employees stop asking questions

- Burnout – Visibly tired employees

- Stress – Anxiety about changes

- Negativity – Prevailing cynicism

- Skepticism – People expressing doubt about change success

Action Tip: Pace change carefully to give employees time to recover. Stop to celebrate successes and give people time to process the change at each phase. This is especially important during large, drawn-out changes with many components. In general, plan to allow more time than you think you'll need.

RESISTANCE TO CHANGE

Managing resistance to change has always played a large role in change management because most organizational change will be met with some level of resistance. However, the degree of that resistance depends significantly on both individual reactions as well as the methods used to manage the change.

While personality and personal circumstances will determine the reaction many individuals have to change, anticipating those reactions and preparing ahead of time can make a significant difference.

Throughout my research on change management, I was struck by the contrast in different cultural approaches to change. In the United States, it's common practice to roll out new processes, ideas, plans, or organizational structural changes first with the expectation that people will align with the change afterward. However, some companies in Japan and in Europe take the opposite approach by influencing the attitudes of key stakeholders before implementing the change. This approach allows them to create advocacy for the change ahead of time to limit resistance. Of course, it's often not possible to avoid resistance entirely, but key stakeholders can act as champions of change to help move the initiative forward and sway workforce attitudes toward acceptance.

Individual mindsets toward change can make the difference between whether an initiative succeeds or fails. Of course, someone's mindset toward change is going to be vastly different depending on what the change is—for example, if your company is moving locations, you'd likely be happy if it shortened your commute but frustrated if it doubled your commute. But beyond the way the particular change affects them, people tend to have a general perception of change as a whole that colors the way they receive change they didn't choose, such as organizational change.

In my 2023 research, I surveyed 1,684 participants using 78 questions to determine perceptions toward change.

People who had a negative versus a positive perception of change indicated the following contrasting sentiments.

POSITIVE PERCEPTION OF CHANGE	NEGATIVE PERCEPTION OF CHANGE
• I feel that I have a number of good qualities	• All in all, I am inclined to feel that I am a failure
• I am able to do things as well as most other people	• I often feel fed up
• When changes are announced, I try to react in a problem-solving mode rather than an emotional mode	• I often suffer from nerves
	• Sometimes I feel miserable for no reason
• I am inclined to try new ideas	• At times I think I am no good at all
• When change happens, I react by trying to manage the change rather than complain about it	• Change frustrates me
	• I am an irritable person
• I take a positive attitude toward myself	• My mood often goes up and down
• I intend to do whatever possible to support change	• I don't like change
• I often suggest new approaches to things	• I usually hesitate to try new ideas
• I usually support new ideas	
• Other people think I support change	

**You can't make someone change.
You can only create an environment that inspires
or motivates people to do something.**

We only have control over our own thoughts and actions. It's up to each individual to choose the attitude or behavior they want to have.

"We cannot change anything until we accept it. Condemnation does not liberate, it oppresses."

—Carl Jung

4

How Can Change Be Successful?

When change is managed well, leaders allow their teams enough space to experience and process the psychological effects of change and help them navigate that process toward acceptance. In contrast, when it's managed poorly, it's common for the leadership team to announce a change and assume that everyone is committed to it, leaving little room for individuals to react, respond, and adapt.

THE THREE STAGES OF EVOLUTION

Because adapting to change is a skill set, some individuals will adapt more quickly than others. However, everyone must go through the psychological steps of that process:

- **Acknowledgement** – The stakeholder learns about the change and begins processing it.

- **Acclimation** – The stakeholder continues to process the change and begins to experiment with new ways of working.

- **Acceptance** – The stakeholder has implemented and adjusted to the change and embraced the new status quo.

We'll cover these stages of evolution in more detail in chapter 6. Each person's journey through the three phases can look different depending on their skill level at adjusting to change and how the change affects them personally.

Excellent change management not only allows people the time and space to move through the phases of change but also facilitates the transition by providing people with the tools and support to navigate the change successfully. Leadership is needed at every level, from the individual employee all the way up to the executive level. Change management is a process that engages with the individual employee, the teams involved, and the organization's culture as a whole.

An example of effective change management came from a merger between two organizations. The purchasing company analyzed all of their employees, around 400 people, to determine the percentage of legacy employees versus new hires after the merger to determine the demographic makeup. They did an excellent job with communication by continuously telling people about the change, where the organization was headed, and where everyone fit into the picture of the new vision.

Best of all, employees were given autonomy and freedom in implementing the change. The management asked the employees for feedback about what they wanted to do differently since they had the opportunity to change their processes as a result of the merger, which invited collaboration and allowed the management to receive valuable input from every level of the organization.

What, then, do you need to manage change excellently? It's all about communication and planning.

VISION AND PURPOSE

It's impossible for change to be successful without a clear vision and purpose. Vision and purpose are necessary to make informed decisions about *what* is changing and *why*. They also serve as a destination around which to build the road map for the change.

If the change is meant to solve a problem, the leaders shaping the change need to know what the problem is and why it occurred in the first place, so they can craft a solution that addresses the root cause. Often this requires research to understand the inner workings and systems within the organization.

ВЫСОЦК
ВЫБОРГ
Соколинское
Гончарово
Перово
СОВЕТСКИЙ
Глебычево
Прибылово
Вещево
Ермилово
Каменка
Красная Долина
Рябово
О. ТВЕРДЫШ
БУХТА ЗАЩИТНАЯ
ВЫБОРГСКИЙ
КИРОВСКИЙ
Кирпичное
Красносельское
Поляны
Семиозерье
Пушное
Победа
Цвелодубово

If the change is to take advantage of an opportunity, which may be the case in an acquisition, leaders need to understand the vision and purpose in order to guide the organization toward success.

Whatever the vision and purpose are, they then need to be communicated to every level of the organization so that everyone understands the reason the change is happening and the desired outcome.

I worked with a manufacturing company that makes extremely expensive water sport products but didn't have a clear vision and purpose. After having seen the way their organization operated, it gave me an understanding of their internal culture, which was conflict avoidant and affected their ability to be nimble and change when needed.

This company had never taken time to define their values or their mission. They made a lot of mistakes, but they never stopped to investigate what went wrong and how to avoid doing those things in the future. It was clear they needed to change the way they did things, but no one engaged the employees to ask for feedback or contribute ideas about how things could be done differently, how to train or develop people, or how to measure success.

One clear sign of chaos was that they would define a metric for performance, and when they didn't meet that metric, they would simply change the goal to something else that they could hit. If the goal was to create something of grade A quality and they didn't hit that, they would simply shift the goal to achieving B grade and be happy when they reached B grade instead.

A company without a vision, mission, purpose, or values will struggle to adapt because they will have nothing to measure themselves against.

When a company doesn't have a clear vision and purpose for the changes they're making, and they haven't taken the time to understand where the problems are, the changes they make can simply be stabs in the dark. They are hoping they hit the right thing and stumble into success—but that's a strategy that will only lead to chaos.

Gathering information is an essential part of any change. It's necessary to pinpoint the causes of problems that need to be solved and to move forward with a clear plan for how to address those things with a full understanding of their working parts. That requires feedback from people involved with the process at every level.

INFORMATION AND INCLUSION

There are two items people want during a change: information and inclusion.

They want the information they need and in the fashion that they want it, whether that's in writing, through a one-on-one meeting, or in a town hall-style meeting. It's impossible to over-communicate about a change, and communicating through multiple channels helps to reach everyone involved in a way that they can easily understand and digest the information.

Successful change requires a clear vision and purpose. Everyone needs to understand why it's happening and what the desired outcome is.

They need to have a shared road map to the envisioned future— and that comes through communication.

Communicate, communicate, communicate, and then communicate again.

The second item is inclusion. People want to feel that they're a part of what's going on and that their expertise and opinions are valued. People who are given the autonomy to voice their thoughts are typically more engaged. Change can be an opportunity to ask, "What would you like to try doing differently? Now is the opportunity to try new things."

Providing opportunities for people to give feedback and share their ideas helps people to get involved in the change and take more ownership and initiative. Encourage people to take risks and pilot new ideas and ways of doing things. This creates collaboration, and it can revolutionize your organization's culture around change.

THE INFORMATION WATERFALL

Using the word "transparency" isn't ideal when discussing change because it creates false expectations. Unfortunately, there's nothing transparent about change. Typically the person at the highest level knows about the change first, and they keep it secret until they

tell the next level of executives. They keep it secret until they tell the next level of management, and so on down the line, each level keeping the change confidential until the information is sent out to the rest of the organization. It's not really possible in many cases to be transparent throughout the organization because some things need to be kept secret while they're in development.

Learning about a change works like a waterfall of information throughout the layers of an organization. And as the information flows down to each layer, the people who have just learned about the change must go through the steps of processing it.

Those who decide on the change get to hear about it first, and they slowly disseminate that information down through the leadership to those who will be enacting the change. It goes from top leadership down to managers, who then tell their people, who then must process it.

" The **single biggest** problem in communication is the illusion that it has taken place. "

—George Bernard Shaw

which cost the company lost revenue both in terms of productivity and also potential lost customers.

If your employees are serving clients or customers, the way they feel about that change can make a direct impact on your revenue. If their work is disrupted, it can lead to a loss of sales or poorer customer service. If there's a metaphorical hurricane going on within your own organization, how will your customer-facing employees be able to focus enough to have conversations with the customer? Will they be able to separate their perception of the change from how they present it to the customer? Will they be able to provide the level of service the customer expects?

CHOOSE LANGUAGE CAREFULLY

The language a company uses around change frames the way that change is perceived. While words and labels may not seem important, they directly affect a team's attitudes and can even create culture, so leaders should be careful in choosing the words they use.

A company in the consumer packaged goods industry went through a merger and the leadership team looked at all of the employees from the new company versus the existing one. They did some research to identify who was with their company and who was coming over from the new company in order to determine who they would need to hire to fill any holes.

The existing employees from the acquired company were called "legacy" employees. And while the leadership team didn't mean for that to carry a negative connotation, it did, because it implied that those people were outdated and might not be committed to the change. People who were new hires or employed with the acquiring organization were viewed more positively than those coming in from the acquired company.

PROCESSING TIME

Give everyone time to process! The most common mistake in change management is not allowing people time to work through the phases of transition: acknowledge, acclimate, and accept. Sometimes change needs to happen rapidly, and in those cases, it is even more important to have champions of change offering support and guiding people through the transition.

Without providing adequate support and processing time, organizations are likely to experience internal conflict, lack of engagement from employees, increased absenteeism, loss of revenue and customers due to interruption, and loss of employees who begin looking for other jobs due to frustration or damaged trust.

Remember that adapting to change is a skill. Every employee has a different level of resilience to change and will respond based on their own behavioral style, personality, and experiences. Becoming a champion of change is about helping them gain the skills to navigate the phases of transition successfully.

"When you're finished changing,
you're finished."

—Benjamin Franklin

5

The Role of Personality and Behavioral Style

During all the change I went through when I worked at one of the world's largest family businesses, I experienced many emotions and saw a wide variety of responses to change around me. It struck me that many of the differing experiences people have when undergoing organizational change were tied to their personalities. It was never something that the company addressed—instead, they simply presented the change, told us our parts in it, and moved forward with implementing it with little to no regard for its effect on people. For some people, it felt like a gut punch. Others were not nearly as fazed, and some even seemed excited by it.

As I began to look at organizational change more closely in my research, I was surprised to find no research on personality or behavioral style in relation to change, which led me to conducting the research myself.

Looking at change through the lens of personality and behavioral style allows leaders to appreciate the similarities and differences in how each person uniquely approaches change.

Change management models often fail because they don't take individual styles into consideration. When doing research, I evaluated 130 different change management models and was surprised to find that only one considered a psychological approach to change, and none of them utilized a behavioral style or personality model to help understand individual responses to change.

Change is not a one-time event—it's a psychological process.

The purpose of behavioral assessments and tools is not to stereotype individuals or put them into boxes—it's simply to help people, especially leaders, understand the individuals better so they can identify their needs and know what to give those people during times of change.

While there are a number of scientific personality and behavior models, for my own research I chose to use the DISC model, which measures observable behavior in four main domains. DISC is a fairly easy and intuitive tool for people to better understand themselves and also better understand others around them.

The DISC model offers a digestible way to understand how people tend to respond to change and identify their needs and desires, which is extremely useful to leaders to facilitate change management. The DISC model identifies specific tendencies that affect how people prefer to work and communicate, as well as how they respond and behave under stress.

For example, under the DISC model, a person with a high D style (dominance) has a need for autonomy and will want to know how they can get involved. The I style (influence) might prefer a team environment where they can have a dialogue around the change, but someone with a S style (steadiness) will likely appreciate a great deal of transparency so they know what to expect. The C style (compliance or conscientiousness) is likely to want a lot of information and details to understand the steps and the system.

If you already have some familiarity with the DISC model, you may be nodding along, but I'll provide a simple explanation for those who aren't familiar with it or need a refresher.

INTRO TO DISC

People have recognized the differences in individuals for thousands of years, but the scientific study of personality and behavior is much more recent. Early thinkers like Hippocrates, Galen, and Aristotle conceptualized the differences they observed among humans in terms of emotions rather than personality. Hippocrates introduced the theory of four humors—blood, yellow bile, black bile, and phlegm—which he believed influenced bodily temperature and health. This theory suggested that the balance of these humors affected a person's temperament, giving rise to terms like "hot-blooded" or "cold-blooded," which referred to one's personality rather than actual body temperature. Galen expanded on this by linking these humors to specific temperaments: sanguine, phlegmatic, choleric, and melancholic. These ideas significantly shaped early discussions on emotions and personality and laid the groundwork for future psychological theories.

Even in ancient times, people attempted to better understand their fellow humans by sorting traits into different domains. Many other scholars furthered the research into personality throughout history and paved the way for the creation of the models we know today, such as DISC, MBTI (Myers-Briggs Type Indicator), or the Enneagram.

DISC theory began with the work of William Moulton Marston. His research was initially an attempt to identify indicators of when someone was lying or telling the truth. He created what became the first lie detector machine. However, to reach that point in his research, he had to examine the emotions of normal people, so he shifted his research to better understand ordinary emotions and behavior. Throughout that research and in his book, *The Emotions of Normal People* (1928), he was able to categorize four domains that became the basis for DISC theory: dominance, influence, steadiness, and conscientiousness (or compliance).

Of course, these domains don't describe all of someone's emotions or behavior, and they only cover four specific aspects of a person's observable behavioral style, but they are very useful in understanding how people tend to behave in relation to those four categories.

> **D** – Dominance measures how someone responds to problems and challenges.
>
> **I** – Influence measures how someone influences people and contacts to their point of view.
>
> **S** – Steadiness measures how someone responds to the pace and consistency of the environment.
>
> **C** – Conscientiousness (or compliance) measures how someone responds to rules and procedures set by others.

The way these personality components are described and measured varies based on different assessments, but understand that no one falls completely in one category or another. We are all made up of each domain to some extent.

Everyone has aspects of each domain, which are expressed differently based on their unique behavioral style.

The domains reflect how an individual responds to people, pace, and consistency in their environment.

DISC is a powerful tool for leaders to understand both their own behaviors as well as the behaviors of their team members. It can help leaders understand behavioral tendencies such as resilience to change, communication preferences and need for information, and motivational drives. Awareness of these differences allows you to tailor your approach to different individuals, and understanding your own behavioral style and personality can help you modify your behavior as necessary.

We'll cover more on DISC and the way different styles tend to respond to change in chapter 7.

" Change is **hardest** at the beginning,
messiest in the middle,
and **best** at the end. "

—Robin Sharma

6

The Three Stages of Evolution

Many change management models approach organizational change from a perspective focused on process rather than psychology.

When I was going through my Ph.D. program at Pepperdine, one of my professors presented a document that contained 130 different change models, and the only model that really focused on the psychological components of change was from William Bridges.

William Bridges' model of change categorizes three zones of change: ending, neutral, and beginning. Change requires the status quo to end, and from there people move into a neutral zone where they're adjusting to or preparing for the new status quo, and finally, the new status quo begins. This is not dissimilar to how I look at the psychological phases of change, with three stages of evolution that represent the psychological process people undergo to process change. My corporate experience, research, and the model from William Bridges inspired me to create this model:

- **Acknowledgment** – The stakeholder learns about the change and begins processing it.

- **Acclimation** – The stakeholder continues to process the change and begins to experiment with different ways of working.

- **Acceptance** – The stakeholder has implemented and adjusted to the change and embraced the new status quo.

Let's take a look at each stage more closely.

ACKNOWLEDGE

Recently, I underwent a transition when my client experience manager gave me her resignation notice. She'd been working for me for nearly a decade, but I knew something would likely change soon because she always wanted to work in higher education and had recently received her master's degree. When she went away on a two-week vacation, she texted me on her second day away and asked to talk, and I knew that she was about to give her notice. I understood it—she had an opportunity to follow her dream and I was supportive, but the reality of the change was still an adjustment.

That day, I told my husband that I was losing her, and he asked me what my plan was now. I replied that my plan was nothing for a couple of days—I just needed to soak the news in, process it, and acknowledge what was going on. During that time, I considered what she did for me and how I would manage those tasks without her. I thought of the aspects of my work that would be immediately different. I had another person who worked part time who could fill the void, but I still felt a sense of loss because this team member had been such a great fit for me and our organization. Eventually, I moved into the acclimation phase when I was able to initiate a plan for taking care of the work that she was previously responsible for and implement solutions.

From a leadership perspective, you must recognize that everyone affected by the change—every stakeholder—needs time to acknowledge the change before they're able to move into acclimation.

So many organizations jump into making changes without giving employees time to process and accept the change, which can create more resistance than necessary as people may be in shock.

Leader Tip: During the acknowledgment stage, leaders should check in with their team members to assess how they are processing the change, provide answers to questions and ensure each person understands the change fully, and offer as much support as they're able.

Individual Tip: Try to be adaptable at the onset of a change. Being adaptable and embracing a change or something new releases dopamine, one of the four feel-good hormones, which will further increase your desire to learn more. (Bromberg-Martin E.S., Matsumoto, M., Hikosaka, O. "Dopamine in motivational control: rewarding, aversive, and alerting." *Neuron*, Dec. 9, 2010.)

HOW TO HELP PEOPLE ACKNOWLEDGE THE CHANGE

- Allow time to process emotions.

- Expect and prepare for strong emotional reactions.

- Give people information again and again.

- Celebrate people and things that are leaving or changing with respect.

- Sell the vision and purpose (the "why").

- Create open lines of communication.

- Identify who is losing what and who is gaining something new.

- Acknowledge the loss openly and empathetically.

- Expect and accept the signs of grieving.

- Let people take a piece of the old way with them.

ACCLIMATE

Webster's dictionary definition of acclimation is "to adapt or adjust to a new temperature, attitude, climate, environment, or situation." Acclimation to a change is the second stage of evolution that describes how someone psychologically acclimates oneself to the change.

The acclimation phase is when people are trying to figure out how they go about doing something differently. It's an opportunity for them to innovate and change, whether they want to or have to.

Sometimes change can be scary because it's charting new waters, and it can carry low or high stakes. For example, if a grocery store decides to rearrange their store with a new layout, that can be very frustrating for people to adjust to, but that's a low-stakes change. At the most, if you're frustrated enough, you might choose to shop at a different grocery store. On the other hand, a business reorganization or merger is a high-stakes, personal, and professional change that deeply affects the lives of the stakeholders. It might mean new leadership, new team members, new products, and many people leaving the organization. A change of that sort tends to require a longer acclimation phase, though how long and difficult the phase is depends on the individual.

How the acclimation phase plays out is also highly dependent on the leader. Are they going to give their people the autonomy and agency to work toward the end result, or are they going to say, "Here are the 10 steps you must follow in this order"?

In some cases, particularly for more technical or process-oriented transitions, everyone simply needs to follow the steps to get something done. But for less structured changes such as cultural changes, there is a need for more autonomy. It's very difficult, and perhaps impossible, to implement cultural changes through process alone. It's even more difficult with older companies, which can have cultures steeped in deep traditions. However, making space for personal autonomy in the acclimation phase can help people to adapt by allowing them to make meaningful choices.

Leaders should continue to check in with their team members regularly throughout the acclimation phase because this is where many problems tend to arise, as it is typically the longest phase. Soliciting feedback during this phase is also important in order to make any necessary adjustments to the process.

The fourth largest electrical contractor in the state of California had five locations throughout the state, and each location was run like its own franchise, with its own departments in finance, operations, purchasing, and more. Each location made its own decisions and did not communicate with the others, and hence silos were created. Some of the company's more notable contracts included performing electrical work for California Adventure, the Arco Towers in downtown Los Angeles, the Golden Gate Bridge in San Francisco, and the MTA blue, green, red, and gold lines.

One employee started out as an entry-level, first-year electrical apprentice and 12 years later obtained the position of executive vice president. The new EVP was 20-30 years younger than some of the other employees, and of course many felt he was not qualified simply due to his age.

The EVP started to implement a plan to create a unified company, which was just the beginning of various massive changes for the organization. One change was the purchase of company vehicles and other commodities. The EVP realized each location was purchasing 20-plus trucks annually, but there was no centralized approval for vehicle purchases or even an attempt to try to buy directly from Ford. So the EVP arranged for a meeting with Ford to commit to an annual number of vehicle purchases and realized price savings in the process.

The EVP admitted that his hardest job was managing personalities. He needed to figure out what drove each person in order to get the most from his people. He was a very hands-on leader and inquired how work was conducted in each department to educate himself about the specific business needs of every department and person in the company, which ultimately resulted in successful change.

During their *acclimation phase*, the EVP was very open to new ideas from his team and gave people the autonomy to try new ways of working. He encouraged the team to share ideas and new approaches. As a result, the new changes created efficiencies, reduced redundancies, and improved cash flow. Eventually the company gained a reputation as *the* company that other electricians wanted to work for.

Leader Tip: Encourage everyone to try something new. Be forgiving when mistakes are made as your team is trying something different. Be approachable and avoid shooting someone's ideas down too quickly.

Individual Tip: Use daydreaming as a strategy to discover new ideas. There has been a long-known connection between daydreaming and creativity. Spend time in nature, on a walk, anywhere not at your normal workspace to encourage new and divergent ideas.

HOW TO HELP PEOPLE ACCLIMATE TO CHANGE

- Acknowledge that it is normal for people to feel unclear about the change.

- Create temporary structures and continuity for this phase.

- Strengthen relationships, new and old.

- Use this phase as a time to promote innovation and an opportunity to try out new things.

- Solicit new ideas from the workforce.

- Use creative problem-solving techniques.

- Step back, take stock, and challenge accepted answers.

- Set short-term milestones.

- Communication is vital. What do people need to know?

- Provide support to people.

ACCEPT

Someone has reached the acceptance phase when they can see what the future will look like, have bought into the agenda, and are enacting their new role with a sense of peace or fulfillment. Not everyone will reach the acceptance phase with every change because not everyone will fully commit to a change. Some people will remain stuck in their old ways, and others will truly accept the change and move on with a sense of peace, happiness, or fulfillment.

Leaders play a role in whether their people are able to reach acceptance, both during the acclimation phase and in the early parts of the acceptance phase. Listening is a big part of that—people need to feel heard.

In his book, *The Five Dysfunctions of a Team*, Patrick Lencioni discusses commitment as one of the dysfunctions. He notes that people need to weigh in with ideas and opinions before they can buy in. So even when you think people have reached acceptance, continue to solicit feedback. As a leader, you may not use what they've said, but you at least need to give them the opportunity to get their thoughts off their chest. People need to feel heard in order to process and accept the change. Once you've heard what they have to say, you can decide what you think is best for the team or the company to move forward.

> " Few, if any, forces in human affairs are as **powerful** as shared vision. "
>
> —Peter Senge

Leader Tip: As the leader, be sure you are loyal to the new direction. Do not agree with your own manager about the change and then speak negatively and gossip about the change to your team.

Individual Tip: Be patriotic toward the change and the new vision or direction the company is going. Help others who may not have reached the acceptance phase to get there with you.

HOW TO HELP PEOPLE ACCEPT THE CHANGE

- Continue to clarify and communicate the process over and over.

- Create a mental picture of the future and the possibilities it holds.

- Create a plan and communicate it to all involved.

- Explain the roles and requirements for everyone.

- Expect a mixture of emotions: positive and resistant.

- Clarify and communicate the purpose of the change.

- After clarifying purpose, communicate the picture of the future.

- Reinforce performance standards.

- Speak and act consistently.

- Slow down to celebrate wins, big and small.

" The **art** of life lies in a constant
readjustment to our surroundings. "

—Kakuzo Okakura

7

How DISC Styles Respond to Change

Someone's strongest DISC style does not 100% determine how they will respond to change, but it can help predict their response and understand how they may process change, what their needs are, and what strengths they bring to the table.

The key factor in how someone will respond to a change is whether they view it as a positive or negative development. This is often influenced by their behavioral style, and people with D and I styles are generally more amenable to change, ambiguity, and risk-taking, while those with S and C styles may be less comfortable with change and the ambiguity and risk involved in it. However, how the change affects someone is often the primary factor that determines their response, and the way they respond from there will tend to correlate with their DISC style.

Different styles tend to process change at different paces. While the D and I styles are likely to embrace change quickly and be ready to move forward at a faster pace, S and C styles generally take longer to process the change and will want as much notice as possible in order to prepare and adjust. That doesn't mean that S and C styles will block change—they may take a little longer to get on board, but when they do, they can be excellent supporters and champions of change.

Understanding the tendencies of the DISC styles in how they relate to change can help leaders identify how to meet their people's needs so they will commit to the change.

My favorite question to identify someone's needs is "Do you want me to hear you, help you, or handle it?" This allows you to identify the kind of support they need. If they want to be heard, they simply need you to be a sounding board and don't need you to offer solutions. If they need help, you can coach them by asking them questions to help them find the answers so they can handle the challenge themselves. And sometimes people need you to simply tell them what to do. What their needs are will often be determined by their behavioral style as well as how they view the change.

D STYLE

People with a D style often see the change from the big picture first rather than considering the details. They aren't overly emotional about change and generally take a matter-of-fact approach. The D style is inclined to take risks and tends to be ambitious and competitive. Under stress, they may come across as tense, irritable, or impatient.

They often enjoy complex problems and ambiguity, and as a result, they usually view change positively.

NEEDS:

- The D style needs others to be direct in communication about the change.

- They prefer others to talk straight and not "beat around the bush."

- If they're allowed to set their own rules or construct their own path forward, they are more likely to embrace the change.

STRENGTHS:

- They usually have a positive view of change, seeing it as a challenge and something to accomplish.

- They often like ambiguity because it gives them autonomy to make decisions and set their own rules and path forward.

- They have a high internal locus of control and feel they are in control of their destiny.

I STYLE

Someone with an I style is naturally positive and optimistic and therefore tends to have a positive view toward change. They have an adventurous and exploratory attitude toward life in general and believe this leads to success in life, with a positive self-image.

The I style typically embraces change and may see it as exciting or invigorating. They tend to make excellent champions of change as their positive perspective can be exceptionally helpful in getting others to commit to the new initiative.

NEEDS:

- Someone with an I style needs to understand the big picture and where are they going with the change to get on board.

- Rather than desiring help, they often simply want their voice to be heard. Inquire about how they're personally doing.

- They desire the support of their teammates or colleagues, so recognition of their efforts is important.

STRENGTHS:

- Individuals with strong I tendencies are naturally positive and are likely to have a positive view toward change since they see it as an exciting adventure.

- Rather than complaining about change, the I style is likely to go into "help mode" and focus on helping others.

S STYLE

People with the S style tend to view change negatively because it causes conflict that upsets social harmony, and they need a sense of harmony in order to feel secure. They're usually uncomfortable with ambiguity, which is inherent to organizational change.

However, the S style is generally steady and agreeable. This can be a benefit as they often won't cause conflict, but they also may not express how they're really feeling because they're hesitant to show negative emotions externally.

NEEDS:

- The S style needs clear expectations about their role during change and all aspects of the change to eliminate as much ambiguity as possible. Clear communication about expectations can help them feel more secure.

- They need to feel appreciated for their efforts in order to feel valued and part of the change.

- Give people with the S style as much notice as possible about the change so they can process and prepare.

STRENGTHS:

- Individuals with the S style have a strong ability to support others and be good sounding boards for others' feelings because of their caring nature.

- They tend to show their appreciation for others during change, which can boost morale and help others commit to the change.

- They take a diplomatic approach to communication and can be strong peacemakers.

C STYLE

Someone with a C style is detail oriented with a strong desire to deliver high-quality work because they identify strongly with their work and believe it reflects directly on them. As a result, they dislike being rushed and may have a tendency toward perfectionism.

Generally, the C style is not inclined to try new ideas or take risks. They are often frustrated by change because it can cause chaos and ambiguity.

NEEDS:

- A person with the C style wants to understand the reason for change. They want to know what was broken in the system that needs to be fixed.

- They prefer to have as much notice about the change as possible in order to properly prepare, especially if they're tasked with enacting something about change, so they can be thorough and accurate.

STRENGTHS:

- Someone with C tendencies is orderly, methodical, and systematic about their approach to change.

- They may challenge the new direction presented by the change because they're trying to be thorough and clear, which can create valuable feedback and help identify problems previously overlooked. They may have ideas about other approaches to solving problems.

- They like to make decisions based on research and data and can be valuable in planning the change successfully.

DISC STYLES AND CHANGE

DOMINANCE

- Tends to have a positive view of change
- Tends to provide positive support to others during change
- Sees change as more interesting than consistency
- May prefer ambiguous situations because it might afford them more autonomy
- Has a higher degree of risk-taking initiative

The D style seeks agency and autonomy.

INFLUENCE

- Usually has a positive view of change, yet as for anyone, bad experiences can cause a shift to a negative view of change
- Goes into help mode once they hear about a change
- Sees changes as new opportunities
- Routine might seem boring to this style, so change may be welcomed

The I style seeks belonging and connection.

STEADINESS

- Tends to have a negative view of change due to their need for harmony
- May have a hard time coping with change
- Tends to dislike ambiguity, which may make them feel uneasy during change
- Does not see themselves as a leader of transformation efforts
- Likely diplomatic in nature and an excellent peacemaker

The S style seeks safety and security.

CONSCIENTIOUSNESS

- Tends to have a negative view of change
- May have a hard time coping with change
- May respond more poorly to stress and have more anxiety and irritability
- Tends to be more risk-averse
- Sees the way to success as being orderly and systematic rather than adventurous and exploratory
- Needs more time to process change

The C style seeks information and systems.

DISC STYLES AT THEIR BEST AND WORST

DOMINANCE

Best
Wants to move the change forward to reach the new goal

Worst
May steamroll others to get their way, leaving team members behind

INFLUENCE

Best
Enthusiastic, positive, and excited about the change

Worst
Overly dramatic and may gossip about the change or those involved

STEADINESS

Best
Listens to others well and seeks to support team members

Worst
Doesn't speak up to share opinions and may explode if they try to keep the "lid" on their feelings for too long

CONSCIENTIOUSNESS

Best
Wants to be thorough to deliver a high-quality output, product, or process

Worst
Irritated or uncomfortable by too many emotions

HOW TO SUPPORT THE DISC STYLES DURING CHANGE

DOMINANCE

Give the D style a road map for the change and the freedom to make decisions along the way. Be direct about the change and don't be overly emotional.

INFLUENCE

Explain to an I style the big picture about where the change is heading first, then create a congenial environment for them. Inquire how they are personally doing during the change.

STEADINESS

Provide the S style with clear expectations to understand what their role is specifically, and give them assurance that others will not be harmed as a result of the change. Show appreciation of their efforts during the change.

CONSCIENTIOUSNESS

For the C style, explain the specific reason for the change, such as what was broken, wrong, or inefficient, as well as how the systems will be improved. Provide them as much advance notice as possible, especially if they are tasked in the execution of the change.

While behavioral style influences the way someone views change in general, an individual's attitude toward a specific change will depend on a variety of variables.

Any behavioral style can become a champion of change.

The most important trait of a champion of change is a positive attitude toward the change. You won't have the same champions of change for every change initiative. Someone who was a fantastic champion for the last change may not feel quite as positive toward the next change.

It can be valuable to have champions of change with all behavioral styles as each brings something unique to the table. Someone with I tendencies might have a higher level of enthusiasm than someone with a C style, and that enthusiasm might inspire other I styles but be overwhelming to a C style. An excellent champion of change will adapt their behavior and energy level to fit whomever they're communicating with. People with strong D and I styles can be very fast paced, even in the way they speak and walk, while C and S styles tend to take things at a more moderate pace. Mirroring someone's manner, to a certain extent, can help to connect with them, so it's important to be socially aware and stretch outside of your comfort zone to help others feel more comfortable.

If someone is aware of what's expected of them and the attributes they need to have, they can modify their behavior to match those traits. The D style is likely to be comfortable with the change quickly and ready to move things ahead at full throttle, but they may need to slow down to ensure they bring other people along with them. A C style will want to be more methodical and take the change at a slower pace, but that may not be what's needed for the change to be successful.

Also keep in mind that someone's primary behavioral style doesn't predict all of their traits, as everyone relates to each style in some way. Someone who has a combination of C and D traits might be both methodical and ready to take risks—you can't assume someone will be risk-averse just because they primarily display C style tendencies. Someone who has strong S tendencies isn't necessarily always averse to conflict—conflict management is a skill they may have developed.

LEADERS AND BEHAVIORAL STYLE

Leaders should also be aware of their own behavioral style and how it affects their leadership through change. This can help them identify what their own strengths and challenges might be.

For example, a D style will likely want everyone else to commit to the change as soon as possible and move at a faster pace than their team might need in that moment. They might be very direct and could be misinterpreted as being blunt or thoughtless.

If you have strong D tendencies, it's important to adapt your approach to account for these things and recognize that others may not be able to process the change as quickly as you expect.

If you have an I style, you might already be focused on the interpersonal needs of the team and empathizing will likely come naturally. But while the change might seem exciting for you, recognize that it may not be exciting for others, so be careful to practice social awareness.

An S-style leader is likely to focus on the safety and security of the team, ensuring everyone is considered and taken care of. This can be difficult for a leader who may know how a change is likely to impact certain team members, which can weigh heavily on their shoulders because of their need for harmony in the environment. Managing conflict during change can also be difficult for an S style leader who tends to avoid conflict in general, which may lead them to put off necessary conversations. Sometimes it's necessary to speak directly and not sugarcoat information.

If you're a leader with a C style, you may feel uncomfortable with the emotions and interpersonal aspects of the change. If someone is in tears in your office, that's likely to be stressful for you. You're probably focused on the facts and details of the change and are more process oriented, but it's important not to overlook the psychological components.

We all have the ability to adapt to situations regardless of our behavioral styles—it's simply a matter of adjusting our approach even when it isn't comfortable. Leaders especially need the ability to flex their style in order to make change successful. Understanding your own tendencies and attitudes toward change and change management can help you lead more effectively as you compensate for those things.

Identifying the behavioral styles of your team members can help you understand how to adjust your leadership approach for various individuals and also help you identify champions of change within your team with a variety of behavioral styles.

" It is not the **strongest** of the species that survives, not the most **intelligent**, but the one most responsive to **change**. "

—Charles Darwin

8

How Personality Drives Behavior

As we discussed in the previous chapter, a person's attitude toward change is first characterized as either positive or negative based on how they will be affected by it, and from there, how they respond to the change is influenced by their behavioral style.

Beyond DISC, there are several personality traits that affect how someone handles change. Two tools that helped me understand people's approaches to change are the Thomas-Kilmann Conflict Mode Instrument (TKI) and the International Personality Item Pool (IPIP), a public-domain collection of items that can be used for personality assessments (https://ipip.ori.org/).

In my research on personality in relation to change, I used the International Personality Item Pool to evaluate various questions and statements and create my own list of change survey questions. Through that process, I identified five aspects of an individual's personality that are related to how they handle change.

To start, I looked at research that had already been validated about people's attitudes toward change and then developed questions along with questions selected from the IPIP collection. From that research, I distilled five personality scales linked to reactions to change.

- Locus of control

- Neuroticism

- Coping

- Tolerance for ambiguity

- Self-efficacy

These five personality scales are affected by your personality style and influence how you handle the three stages of change—

acknowledge, acclimate, and accept. They correlate with your DISC style, which affects how you relate to change, and that affects how you process each phase of the change.

The first factor that will determine how someone responds to change is whether they view the change as positive or negative. That informs the attitude they will have, which may have something to do with their personality but it could also depend on how they're personally affected by the change and other factors in their life.

In general, people tend to categorize change in one of those two ways: positive or negative. From there, how they respond will be influenced by how they relate to the five personality scales, which inform their attitudes toward change. And all of these factors are influenced by their DISC behavioral styles. The graphic below shows how the five scales contribute to attitudes toward change, and each scale is then described in more detail.

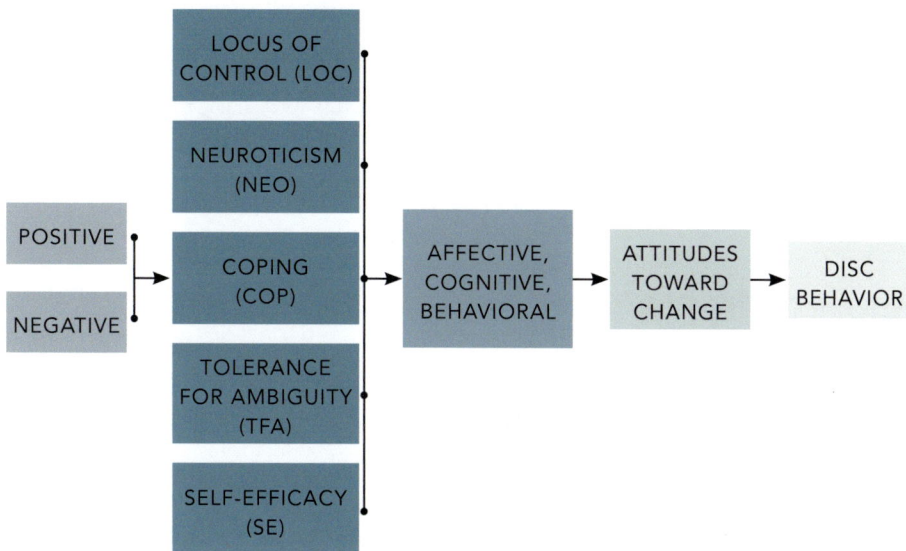

LOCUS OF CONTROL (LOC)

NEUROTICISM (NEO)

POSITIVE

COPING (COP)

AFFECTIVE, COGNITIVE, BEHAVIORAL → ATTITUDES TOWARD CHANGE → DISC BEHAVIOR

NEGATIVE

TOLERANCE FOR AMBIGUITY (TFA)

SELF-EFFICACY (SE)

LOCUS OF CONTROL

Locus of control measures the extent to which someone feels they have control over their life and circumstances. Are you the type of person who tends to feel that things are always happening *to* you, or do you feel that you have control and can change things?

The locus of control scale moves from internal to external. Someone with an internal locus of control feels they have a high level of control over their life and circumstances—their sense of control comes from *within*. Someone with an external locus of control tends to feel that life happens to them and they don't have the power to change things—their sense of control is based on *external* factors.

People with an internal locus of control might be characterized as more active while those with an external locus of control might be characterized as more passive. In general, people who perceive they have more control over their circumstances tend to view change more favorably, and those with an external sense of control are more likely to have a "victim" mindset or feel negatively toward the change. Where someone falls on this scale will not only affect their attitude but also how they cope with the change.

NEUROTICISM

The neuroticism scale describes someone's level of emotional stability—people with higher neuroticism tend to have higher levels of stress and anxiety. The term "neurosis" was coined by Freud to describe emotional or mental suffering, and is often used to describe the experience of negative emotions. People high in neuroticism tend to react more intensely to change, while those low in neuroticism tend to be calmer and have fewer negative thoughts.

Someone with a high level of neuroticism might be perfectionistic or easily frustrated, which can make it more difficult for them to cope with the stressful events associated with change. Someone with low neuroticism is better able to cope with change and is likely to be more tolerant of others' shortcomings.

COPING

Coping describes your direct response to an emotion, the cognitive and behavioral responses you use to manage or tolerate what is going on. If you're going through a change and feel afraid of that change, your emotional response might be avoidance. If you're angry about the change, you may want to lash out in some fashion. On a cognitive level, coping can look like suppression, denial, rationalization, or problem-solving.

Someone who has strong coping skills is better able to regulate their emotions during stressful situations. Someone who does not is more likely to let their emotions get the best of them and the cognitive and behavioral effects of that emotion will become evident.

TOLERANCE FOR AMBIGUITY

Tolerance for ambiguity is a skill set that describes someone's comfort level with the unknown, and it can be difficult to acquire for certain personality types. However, organizational change creates a lot of uncertainty, chaos, and confusion, so tolerance for ambiguity is quite valuable during times of change. Someone with a high tolerance for ambiguity is better able to adapt to different situations and remain flexible while having limited information.

SELF-EFFICACY

Self-efficacy is the perception a person has about their ability to do something in a future scenario, their ability to impact their own motivation and choose their behavior to achieve positive outcomes.

Self-efficacy is made of up three different areas, called the *ABCs of change*:

- Affective – Thoughts and emotions about the change

- Cognitive – Beliefs and opinions about the change

- Behavior – Actions for or against the change

The ABCs of change describe how a person relates to change. Someone's thoughts and emotions about whether a change is positive or negative will inform their perspective about the change. From there, they will form beliefs and opinions about the change based on those feelings. Finally, those things will inform their actions.

THE ABCS OF CHANGE

While an individual may not be able to control how they feel about a change, especially initially, everyone has influence over their thoughts and can choose their behaviors.

For people who have a negative reaction to change and tend to struggle more to adapt, leaders should make an effort to understand where those individuals are coming from and meet their needs, to help them adapt as smoothly as possible. If someone has a low tolerance for ambiguity, it can be much easier for them to commit to a change when their role is very clearly laid out with expectations, guidelines, and steps. In general for DISC, S and C styles tend to be more risk-averse than D and I styles and therefore may struggle to adapt to change.

DISC AND THE THREE PHASES OF CHANGE

The five personality scales relate to how each DISC style responds to change in each of the three stages of evolution: acknowledge, acclimate, and accept.

D (DOMINANCE)

During the acknowledge phase of change evolution, the D style will likely feel equipped to navigate the change themselves. They may be more comfortable with ambiguity as a result of a change because it can provide autonomy as they enter into the acclimate phase. The D style, although direct, may support others positively through the change to help other individuals reach acceptance. The D style might eagerly await the next change so they can conquer the next challenge. They like to tackle tough problems and often find that changing conditions create a more exciting way of life.

I (INFLUENCE)

The I style during the acknowledge phase may have a positive outlook of the change. This positivity will serve them well as they move through the acclimate phase, until they reach acceptance of the change. They are likely to try new ideas and not feel that change is inhibiting them. Like the D style, they may have some comfort with ambiguity and find the newness of the change to be thrilling. Their positivity rarely lets them feel as though they are a failure and on the whole they will tend to feel satisfied with themselves during change. As they and others around them reach acceptance, their upbeat nature will enable them to support others.

S (STEADINESS)

The S style during the acknowledge stage may tend to be more standoffish about change. At the onset, the idea of having to tackle something new might feel more draining than stimulating in comparison to the D and I style. Due to the S style's need for harmony, the acclimate stage may leave them feeling a bit unsettled by the change. Once the S style feels safe and secure about the change, they may move through the acceptance stage more easily.

C (CONSCIENTIOUSNESS)

As the change is announced in the acknowledge phase, the C style may think that orderly and systematic people will go further in the world than their counterparts who just jump into change. The C style likely does not look forward to the next change that might be just down the road. In the acclimate phase, the C style may resist trying new ideas. Allowing the C style the time to understand the need for the change and how their part contributes to the success of the change is necessary and can help lead the C style into the acceptance stage. The C style's need for understanding may present as asking questions, which may be viewed by others as not embracing change even if that is not the case. Once the C style understands the new rules of the change, they are often committed to those rules.

While there are common ways that each DISC style responds to change and engages with the change during each phase, every individual has a unique relationship with the change and may view it differently.

This information can be useful to leaders in predicting how individuals may react so they can more effectively address issues to lead through the phases of transition, but it's important not to assume what any individual feels. Communication must come first.

"Change is **inevitable**.
Growth is **optional**."

—John C. Maxwell

9

Exploring the Change Curve

While not everyone will react negatively to change, for those who do, they often must process the change similarly to processing a loss. Leaders should recognize that organizational change often does cause a sense of loss for many stakeholders, and real losses are often involved with change, whether that's losing one's role, valued coworkers or colleagues, plans that can no longer come to fruition, or simply one's routine.

In her book *On Death and Dying*, Elizabeth Kübler-Ross presents her five-stage model of processing grief based on her research, which has become known as "the change curve."

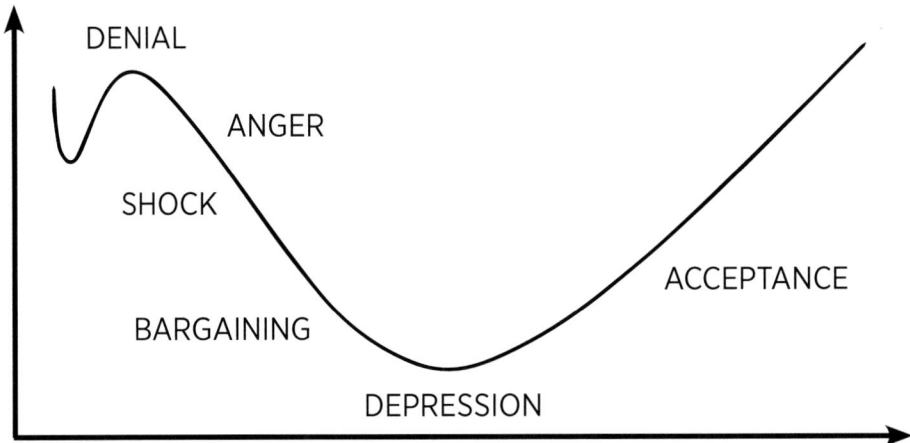

The five stages are as follows:

1. Shock/denial

2. Anger

3. Bargaining

4. Depression

5. Acceptance

Let's look closer at these five stages.

SHOCK/DENIAL

This stage is characterized by disbelief or shock. People may not accept the change initially, and if they stay in this stage too long, it can become harmful to the change initiative. In order to process the change, they must first accept the news they've been given and whatever loss is involved, whether that's a colleague leaving, a company being sold, or a department moving. From there, healing from the loss can begin.

Shock and denial can also take the form of surprise or disbelief, positive or negative. Someone might think, "I never thought this could happen to me." That reaction is likely largely dependent on the kind of change.

This phase can also include confusion. People may have different ideas about what the change will look like, they could have heard about it at different times or from different sources, or they may have interpreted the words differently. Confusion can significantly slow down the change initiative, so excellent and consistent communication is vital during the early phases.

ANGER

It's understandable for people to feel angry at change being thrust upon them. Show empathy and let them experience this emotion fully. Anger is often characterized as a highly negative emotion, but it's a natural part of the process and often must be expressed in order to move past it. Leaders should offer opportunities to appropriately express anger by listening empathetically and not in a condescending way, which will only make people angrier. Empathy is the most powerful way to diffuse anger and help the individual process it to move on to other emotions.

BARGAINING

This stage involves trying to negotiate or play "what-if" games that don't lead to practical solutions. People may feel hopeless or helpless in this stage and are trying to find ways to regain control. People may try to bargain with themselves, their bosses, or even God. Behavior when someone is bargaining may seem to be irrational. Listening during this stage is valuable, but it's important to remain firm about the change.

DEPRESSION

People may feel down, helpless, or hopeless. It's essential to go through this emotion instead of avoiding it, but it's easy to dwell too long in this stage. Leaders should watch out for signs of depression and give support to individuals experiencing this phase to help them move past it.

Other emotions people may experience during this phase are fear and worry. They're thinking about the negative effects the change will have on them, their family, and their teammates. Stress levels are high, with more cortisol in the body, which creates high blood pressure. Fear can even cause people to leave the organization, so it's important that they don't dwell for too long in anxiety.

Emotions can be contagious, and whether someone is angry, fearful, or depressed, those emotions are often very visible to teammates. The last thing you want as a leader is for others to "catch" those negative emotions.

ACCEPTANCE

In this final stage, individuals come to terms with the new reality and can move forward. It doesn't necessarily mean they are happy, but they agree to accept the change.

The change curve can be broken down into a more detailed process, though not everyone will experience all stages of the curve. You can envision this curve plotted on two axes: emotion (from pessimism to optimism) and time (from current to later).

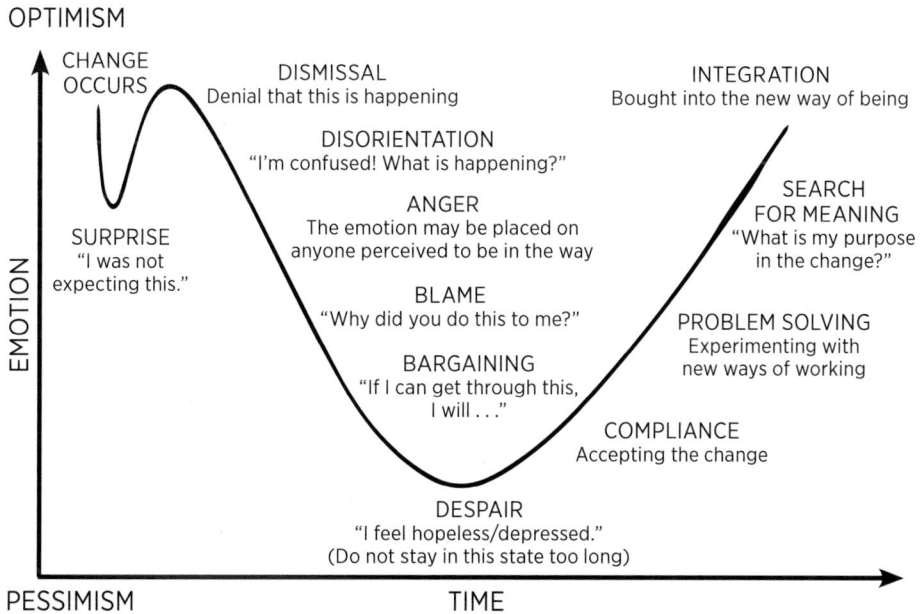

OPTIMISM

CHANGE
OCCURS

DISMISSAL
Denial that this is happening

INTEGRATION
Bought into the new way of being

DISORIENTATION
"I'm confused! What is happening?"

ANGER
The emotion may be placed on
anyone perceived to be in the way

SEARCH
FOR MEANING
"What is my purpose
in the change?"

SURPRISE
"I was not
expecting this."

EMOTION

BLAME
"Why did you do this to me?"

PROBLEM SOLVING
Experimenting with
new ways of working

BARGAINING
"If I can get through this,
I will . . ."

COMPLIANCE
Accepting the change

DESPAIR
"I feel hopeless/depressed."
(Do not stay in this state too long)

PESSIMISM

TIME

How someone experiences the change curve varies significantly from person to person based on their behavioral style, personality, and skill at handling change, as well as their perspective on the change. Do they see the change as positive or negative? Who is creating the change, and do they have respect for that person?

When a change is announced, it causes a disruption and usually results in some kind of shock. Change that's perceived in a more negative way typically takes longer to process, and people need to go through a variety of phases.

Not everyone will view change negatively, and so they may not experience the change curve in the same way. Instead, they may skip over certain phases entirely or move through the phases at a much faster rate, sometimes even in a matter of minutes, like a speed bump before that person is able to move on. However, for some people, it can take days or even months to fully move through the change curve.

For those who struggle more to adjust, they're likely to spend more time ruminating. The change curve is regressive, meaning people may move forward on the curve, and then something could happen that causes them to move back on the curve. However, at some point, they will need to reach acceptance. The goal should be to get through the change curve as quickly as possible and help others to do the same.

Someone who remains on the change curve indefinitely can become a squeaky wheel that's toxic to the organization. A negative attitude from one team member can sway those who are on the fence toward the negative, and those who are managing the change in a positive way will view them as a blocker to change.

Leaders need to not only understand the change curve but also what each member of their team is like and how they can support them during times of change. DISC can be an especially helpful starting point.

Every level of an organization must undergo the change curve, from the change-makers to the team members at the bottom of the organization. This is part of what often makes change chaotic. Perhaps it begins with the C-suite, who then tells everyone in the IT department because they're privy to what needs to be rolled out—now everyone in the IT department must undergo the change curve. The news then needs to be broken to other departments, who also must process the change. Whether things are rolled out in a waterfall or all at one time, it's still going to be disruptive, and time will be needed to process the change.

When everyone in the organization understands the change curve, it fosters better communication among coworkers, managers, and teams.

Here are some important steps to master the change curve.

Communicate the change early and often: Communication is one of the most common places where change management fails, and communicating with people frequently helps ensure they're getting the information they need when they need it. Take people's communication preferences into account and communicate in a variety of ways.

Show empathy: Empathy is essential to effectively lead people through the change curve. Empathy can be challenging to master, especially if it's not a natural skill. Think of empathy like a muscle— the more you use it, the stronger it gets. Empathy involves listening, withholding judgment, and not overreacting. Remember that everyone has different backgrounds and experiences, so be patient as they experience various emotions and adjust to the change.

Offer support: Leaders should reassure their team members as best they can and offer support and solutions wherever possible, yet they need to remain honest about what's happening. Ask each person what they need and keep checking in on their progress. Support might look different for each individual—some might just need someone to listen, while others might need training on specific topics.

Celebrate success: Often, leaders intend to celebrate milestones or achievements but other things get in the way, and the celebration never happens. Celebration plays an important role in overall morale. Slow down, celebrate, and enjoy the feeling of accomplishment before moving on to the next task.

Author Paul Zak, in his book *The Trust Factor*, describes ovation, "which recognizes colleagues who contribute to the organizations success." The idea of ovation provides a release of dopamine, a mood-boosting hormone. Take the thought of ovation one step further and recognize someone for a task completed when it is unexpected, and the impact of dopamine intensifies.

"The most difficult thing is the decision to **act**; the rest is merely tenacity. The fears are paper tigers. You can do **anything** you decide to do."

—Amelia Earhart

10

Facilitating the Change Curve

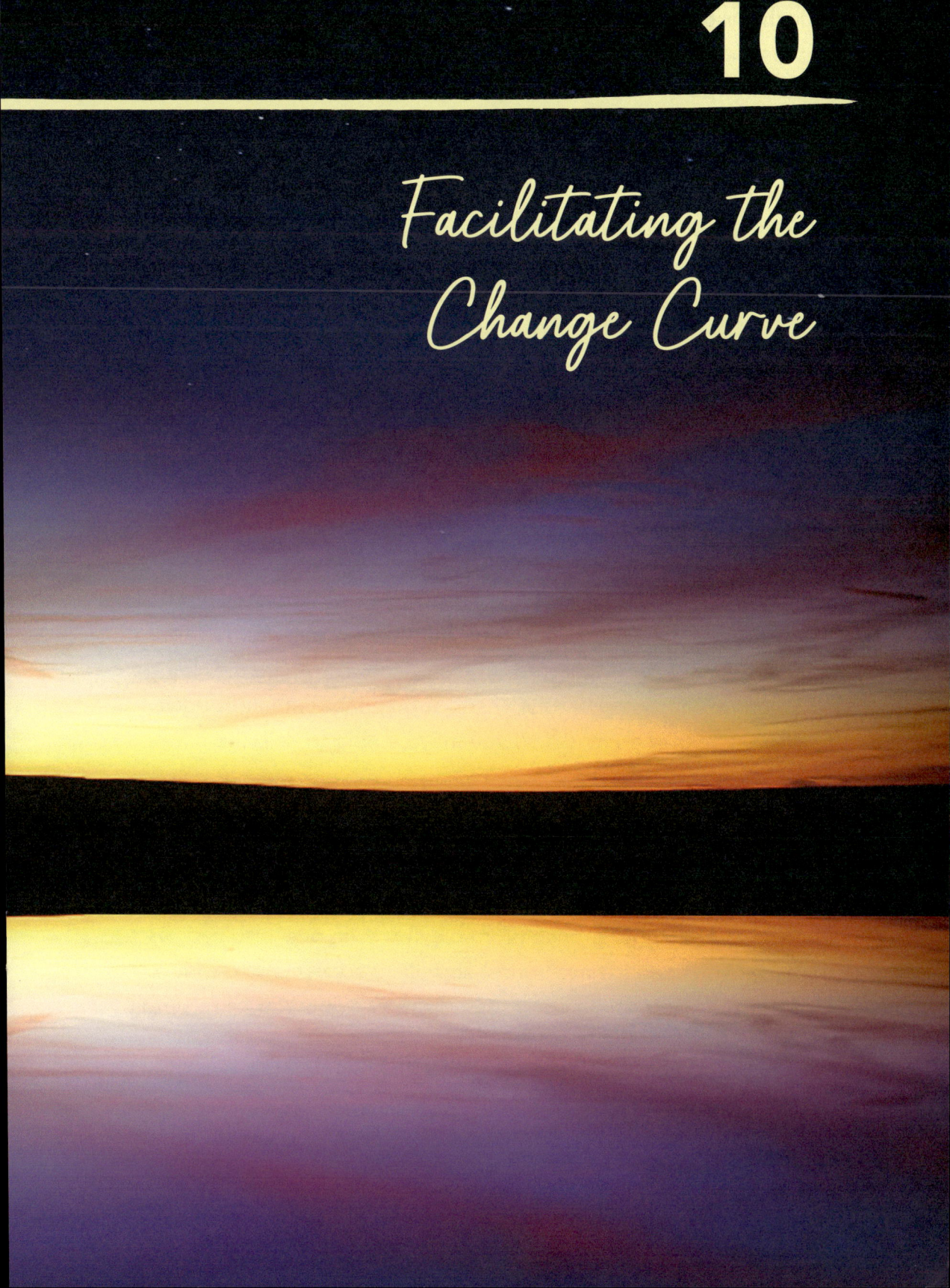

In the last chapter, we discussed the change curve, which describes the emotions people may experience when undergoing change. To help people move through the change curve, it's helpful to know their DISC style and how they may behave in each of the phases. For example, while a D style may be straightforward about how they feel, a C style individual may not show their emotions and just put their head down and grind through it. An S style wants to have harmony in the workplace, and they likely won't say how they feel either. The I style might see change as a shiny new object that is exciting and fun. It comes down to knowing your people and their regular behavior so you can monitor for changes, which requires social awareness.

Leaders should observe body language and general behavior. If someone is usually upbeat and doesn't have the same pep as usual, that could be a red flag that they're struggling. Leaders need to stay approachable and inquire.

Understanding where your team members are in relation to the change curve is the first step in helping them navigate the change. I recommend doing regular check-in meetings with individuals to see where they are and how you may be able to help them.

Change and conflict go hand in hand.
They are two sides of the same coin.

Even if a change is uncomfortable for everyone involved, as a leader you need to have honest and direct conversations with your team members about what they disagree with. You can't simply ignore it.

Kevin Cashman's book *The Pause Principle* explains the importance of slowing down in order to speed up. Taking your time to answer questions and manage the change well from the beginning prevents obstacles that would slow the change by complicating it later on.

Leaders should approach change slowly from the beginning to get as much buy-in as possible. Address problems early. Maybe there's a misunderstanding, or maybe someone has ideas or input that would be useful to hear.

Inevitably, there will be some people who are against the change. But much resistance can be prevented if leaders have conversations with their own teams and with individuals to give everyone a sense of security and the ability to respond freely.

CHECK-IN DIAGNOSTIC

Make a point of meeting with each team member on an individual basis to check in with how they're processing the change. First of all, you want to understand what they're struggling with. It's up to the individual to identify when they can help themselves and where they need assistance.

> " When we are no longer able to **change** a situation, we are challenged to **change** ourselves. "
>
> —Viktor Frankl

This check-in meeting serves as both a diagnostic tool and an opportunity to connect, listen, and create more buy-in by helping the stakeholder process their feelings, understand themselves better, and feel heard. It should be a one-on-one meeting where you set aside about an hour to allow time for the conversation to develop fully—if you don't end up using all of that time, that's fine. I would recommend holding it in a neutral location, somewhere other than your office, such as a conference room or somewhere off-site like a coffee shop. The reason for this is to keep your office a positive space.

This conversation has the potential to turn negative, and you don't want to create a negative emotional connection with your office, because every time that person comes into your office, they may have feelings that put them in a negative frame of mind.

Start with an open-ended question like "Help me understand your point of view about the change." Then be quiet and listen.

Next ask, "Can you tell me more?" I love this question. It is like priming the pump. Ask multiple times until the person says, "I think that's it." You'll be surprised how much more someone might say if you give them the space to do so.

In Michael Bungay Stanier's best-selling book *The Coaching Habit,* he shares seven questions that would be excellent to use in a one-on-one check in:

1. What's on your mind? (This is a great question to kick-start the conversation.)

2. And what else? (This functions similarly to "tell me more.")

3. What is the real challenge here? (This question helps the other person focus.)

4. What do you want?

5. How can I help?

6. If you are saying yes to this, what are you saying no to?

7. What was most useful to you?

Avoid the word "why." It tends to make people defensive. If you ask, "Why are you having a hard time with this change?" They may feel uncomfortable and want to defend their point of view. There's an inherent judgment in that question. Instead, you want to create an open space for them to identify what they're feeling.

Some people may have difficulty expressing their feelings, so let them take their time, and try not to interrupt or ask guiding questions. Your role is to listen to the best of your ability, even if you disagree with them. This is not the time to contradict what they're saying—instead, take whatever they say as valuable information about how they're relating to the change.

Next, ask questions like, "What can I do to make this better?" Obviously, there are limitations to what you can do—certain things just aren't going to happen. You can narrow this down with questions like these:

- What specifically do you need from me?

- How can I be of support to you?

Keep your questions open-ended in order to get as much information as possible. If you ask closed-ended questions, you'll get yes-or-no responses, which don't allow you to learn as much from the team member.

Some yes-or-no questions can be valuable if they lead into important discussions. You might ask, "Do you understand your role and how it fits into the new vision for the organization?" If it's a yes, ask them to explain it to you to verify that you have the same understanding, and if it's a no, that tells you they need clarification from you. You might follow up with, "What pieces can I clarify for you?"

Remember that it's just a conversation. Try to stay calm. The emotion that you exude will often be mirrored by the other person. Keep your body language open.

CHECK-IN QUESTIONS

1. Help me understand your point of view about the change.

2. What specifically do you need from me?
   How can I support you?

3. Do you understand your role and how it fits into the new vision for the organization?

4. What pieces can I clarify for you?

Continue to circle back with individuals multiple times throughout the change. Ask how they're doing and whether they have any new thoughts or if anything has changed since the last time you talked.

This may seem like a lot of work for leaders who have large departments they oversee. For this reason, leaders at every layer of the organization need to be involved in the change management process in order to stay in touch with individuals at every level.

CRAB MODEL

Adapting to change requires agility, which is a skill set that can be developed. While everyone will have an initial response to a change that may be out of their control, they do have the power to choose their attitude as they work through the change. The CRAB model can be a helpful tool for your team to choose their attitude toward change, and it can be used both in one-on-one conversations during a change initiative as well as in preparation for change to help people choose the way they frame the change.

Crabs are built with the ability to easily move in any direction from their current position—sideways, forward, backward. They're able to adjust direction based on the needs of the situation.

"If you don't like something, change it. If you can't change it, change your attitude."

—Maya Angelou

The CRAB model is composed of four elements:

C – Change. What is the change, challenge, or disruption?

R – Resilient response. What is your resilient response to the change?

A – Attitude. What is your attitude toward the change?

B – Behavior. What behavior are you going to adopt in response to the change?

The model begins with understanding the change and from there, people have the opportunity to choose their responses to change.

Ultimately, all you can really control is your own attitude and behavior.

This model helps you identify the right mindset you should have about a change and take responsibility for your actions. It's a tool to help you reflect on what you have control over.

In my change workshops, I like to walk people through a simple thought exercise that is an entry point to the CRAB model. You can use this with your own team members and also for yourself when processing a change.

1. Think of a past situation where change occurred. What was the change?

2. What was your response in that situation?

3. What was your attitude toward the change or challenge?

4. How did you behave?

Reflecting on a past situation can help to put a current change into perspective and gain some emotional distance that makes it easier to choose how you respond. After reflecting on a past experience, examine the current change with the intent to choose your resilient response, attitude, and behavior. This can be especially effective during the early acknowledgment phase of transition, when people are still processing the change and determining their attitudes toward it.

I worked with a major entertainment company and conducted several sessions on change. These sessions were open-enrollment workshops where any employee could sign up. As a result, the workshops had participants who did not know each other.

One of the activities was to get people to reflect by asking about a recent major change they went through using six discussion questions about the change. One participant had three other teammates in this particular session. After the reflective activity, she asked if she could share her response. She said she wanted to take advantage of being able to verbalize her change scenario as a therapeutic response to help her heal.

She went on to share how her husband of 37 years had stage four colon cancer. She realized how much he did for her when he could no longer do any of those things. She shared how much her day-to-day living had changed over the past eight months. Her three teammates were shocked that she had been coming in to work for the past eight months and no one at work knew about this in her life. She closed by sharing that she did not want anyone else, especially her own boss, to think that she could not do her job. She knew what her husband's fate would be and she would need her job in the future.

CHANGE FITNESS TEST

You can utilize a change fitness test during or ahead of each one-on-one conversation to get an idea of the attitude an individual has toward the change as well as what areas they may be struggling with or where they may excel. This can also be a useful tool to help you recognize potential champions of change, and you can use your one-on-one meetings to help those champions understand their role in advocating for change among their teams.

The scores on the test are somewhat subjective, but in general, if someone answers a 9 or higher, you know they're committed and ready for the change, at least in that category. If they score a 6-8, they may need help but are possibly ready for the change. If they answer a 5 or below, they're not ready for the change.

Note: If a leader's team achieves low scores across the board, he or she might do some self-assessment. Perhaps the leader has failed to adequately communicate the change and its necessity.

CHANGE FITNESS TEST

Strongly disagree (1) to strongly agree (10)

	Statement	1	2	3	4	5	6	7	8	9	10
1	I fully understand the vision we are heading toward.										
2	I can explain the change to others on my team, department, or organization.										
3	I understand what my role is in the change.										
4	I am inspired by the change.										
5	I believe the change will make our organization better.										
6	I have the skills needed to make the change successful.										
7	My peers have the skills needed to make the change successful.										
8	I believe my peers are inspired by the change.										
9	I believe my manager is inspired by the change.										
10	I have enough support from others to manage the change.										

The change fitness test can also be used as a survey of a team or the entire organization to determine the group's readiness for change before it happens. To assess group readiness, everyone should fill it out anonymously.

TRACKING STAKEHOLDER PROGRESS

Other surveys can be used to explore how a change affects various stakeholders. Consider tracking stakeholder progress by using a summarizing chart such as the one below.

STAKEHOLDER ANALYSIS
1 (not much) to 5 (critical)

Name of Stakeholder	DISC Style	How critical are they to the success of the change? (1-5)	How does the change affect this person?	How much effort might be needed from this individual? (1-5)	What is the level of commitment this individual has toward the change? (1-5)
Joe Smith	S	5	Dislikes ambiguity and conflict, wants everyone to be valued and secure in their jobs	5	2

List the individuals on your team and ask the following questions about each person:

- **What is their DISC style?** The purpose is to appreciate their similarities and differences and not stereotype or pigeonhole people.

- **How critical are they to the success of the change?** Is their role vital to implementation, or do they hold significant social capital?

- **How does the change affect this person?** In what ways will the change affect their role, their routine, their interests, their career, and their personal life?

- **How much effort might be needed from this individual?** What specifically are you asking them to do? Will they need to significantly adapt their behavioral style to meet those expectations, such as asking an S or a C style to deal with a lot of ambiguity?

- **What is the level of commitment this individual has toward the change?** This is best determined by having a one-on-one conversation with the person. Avoid making assumptions; seek to gain the facts.

Organizational change will affect each person differently depending on their behavioral style, personality, and circumstances. The stakeholder analysis gives leaders a visual representation of areas and people they may need to pay attention to. If someone has a low level of commitment but is critical to the success of the change, that's someone the leader should be checking in with regularly and investing time and resources to help them commit to the change.

Managers at every level can use the stakeholder analysis to visualize and better understand their direct reports. Once the change has occurred or is underway, they can use **stakeholder behavior analysis** such as with the chart below to monitor how team members are handling the change and identify areas where help may be needed.

STAKEHOLDER BEHAVIOR ANALYSIS

Name of Stakeholder	DISC Style	What is the regular behavior I observe?	What is the behavior I observe since the change?	If behavior is negative, what needs to be improved?	Who could be a mentor?

Similar to the stakeholder analysis, write down the names of all your team members and their DISC styles, then answer the following questions for each person:

- **What is the regular behavior I observe?** This can be answered before the change begins, and leaders need to know their direct reports well enough to recognize their regular behavior. Write down a few key personality traits and behaviors.

- **What is the behavior I observe since the change?** Is their behavior any different since the change? Don't focus only on work performance—keep in mind things like energy levels, social interactions, and other factors that can be clues about how the person is feeling.

- **If the behavior is negative, what needs to be improved?** Not everyone will have a negative reaction to the change, but for those who do, identify what needs to change. Maybe the individual seems depressed—then perhaps their mood and ability to cope need to be improved. Maybe the individual is struggling to keep up with their workload, and they could use some guidance or resources. This question can open up understanding about the cause of the negative behavior, but it starts by identifying where the individual currently is and where you'd like them to be.

- **Who could be a mentor?** The best mentors are likely to be champions of change within your team, but it could also be you, the leader.

By keeping track of behavioral changes among your team, you'll be able to see how they progress through the change curve.

"Every great dream begins with a dreamer. Always remember, you have **within you** the strength, the patience, and the passion to reach for the stars to change the world."

—Harriet Tubman

11

How to Become a Champion of Change

Champions of change are the individuals in an organization who are able to quickly adapt to change and help others commit to the change and move the initiative in a positive direction. While leaders should strive to be champions of change, a champion of change can be anyone—and it's best to have champions on every team and at every level of the organization.

What does a champion of change look like?

- Someone who is interested in doing new or different things

- Someone determined to ensure the initiative is successful

- Someone who has the ability to adapt and see things from various angles

- Someone who is enthusiastic about change

- Someone who is empathetic through change

- Someone who has the ability to meet others where they are and offer support

- Someone who paints the picture of a good future

- Someone who is able to get others to participate more effectively

Champions of change are the individuals with more resilience and the ability to keep positive momentum. When teams begin to get tired or frustrated, the champions are the folks who help people get from point A to point B.

During all of the reorganizations I experienced at my previous employer, I always saw myself as a champion of change. Initially, I tried to help people make sense of what was going on, like a crossing guard trying to get everyone safely onto a bus because we needed to move from one location to the next.

As part of my role in sales, I felt the need to always know people in different departments in order to get things done. This strategy enabled me to help others make those connections themselves, which came in useful when people were moved around between departments through reorganizations.

I've also been in need of a champion of change and experienced the difference it can make when someone takes on that role. When I was an adjunct professor at California State University, Fullerton, I started out teaching Advanced Business Communication. Later, I taught some additional sales and marketing classes. I thought it would be useful to create a new minor in sales, yet several of the staff members thought it would infringe on the marketing department because some of the courses overlapped for the sales and marketing minors.

The director of the Sales Leadership Center went to bat to help me sell the idea of creating a sales minor. Every meeting that occurred to discuss the sales minor was a result of his efforts as he tried to get the marketing department chairperson to agree to the idea. We both met often with the marketing chair to continue to rally his support and communicate the progress in getting the new sales minor set up.

Being a champion of change requires a focus on people and a bit of empathy. In the case of the director, he championed change for me by saying to the marketing department, "I understand this is how you might feel about marketing classes being impacted, but think about how this program could benefit the students."

A champion of change views change as an opportunity. Leaders can identify champions of change within their teams, people they know are open-minded or positive influences within their spheres, and tap them on the shoulder to ask for their help to lead the initiative. As the change rolls out, people who are excited about the change often make great candidates for champions of change. People who want to participate should be given the opportunity.

By identifying people who are interested in participating or who may have social influence to help others get on board, you can make them aware of their role in promoting the change.

The first task a champion of change (CoC) needs to do is learn everything they can about what the change is, how it aligns with the organization's goals, and how to communicate those things to others.

From there, their role is to create a supportive environment to help others buy in to the change. That can take a variety of forms depending on the champion's personality and behavioral style. S and I styles will find this natural, but D and C styles can still work toward creating supportive environments. Support can come in a variety of forms, like personal encouragement, clear communication, and help with processes.

D-style champions are likely to be excited about moving the change forward as fast as possible and getting results. They need to be careful to slow down long enough to bring others with them.

I-style champions are excellent at creating enthusiasm and optimism about the change. However, they need to avoid glossing over issues people may be dealing with, as that can create resentment.

S-style champions want harmony and will go out of their way to ensure consensus among people. They need to watch out for any sense of disagreement that may keep them from communicating directly because they wish to avoid conflict.

C-style champions tend to focus on processes and can be great communicators to ensure details are accounted for as well as pointing out advantages and disadvantages of a strategy. They can sometimes overlook the emotional and psychological aspects of the change, so they need to pay attention to how people are feeling.

"Courage is the power to let go of the familiar."

—Raymond Lindquist

Champion of Change Key Attributes				
Attribute	**Definition**	**Who Embodies This Attribute?**	**DISC Style**	**Notes**
Drives for Results	Has a sense of urgency to move the project forward. Is able to marshal the appropriate resources and people to create positive momentum.			
Influence	Has a positive outlook on the change and can convey the vision in a positive fashion so others understand their roles.			
Social Awareness/ Empathy	Has excellent social awareness and relationship management. Inquires how others are doing, listens without passing judgment, and is able to meet others where they are to provide support.			
Credibility	Is seen by others as credible or an expert. Can be counted on and has the utmost integrity. Is thorough and does not take shortcuts.			

Ideally a champion of change would have a little bit of each attribute, but it's likely you will find champions who have strengths in particular areas.

There's benefit to having champions of change of all behavioral styles, as they tend to complement each other. Some individuals will have an easier time navigating certain types of changes and will struggle more with other types of changes based on how they view the particular change—positively or negatively.

Everyone also has the ability to adapt their styles to meet the needs of a situation, and being aware of the behavioral styles of others makes it easier to adjust to their preferences and communicate more effectively.

In order to become a champion of change, you must truly buy into the change.

When some leaders disagree with upper management, they might deflect by saying, "The management wants us to do it this way. I realize it's a bad idea, but we'll try to accommodate them." However, doing this gives away their authority and leadership by deferring to those above them rather than taking ownership of the change.

Being committed to the change doesn't mean you will never have a bad day or get stuck in the change curve. We all have to process change, and that can be difficult for anyone. But you must be able to pick yourself up and march forward so your team can follow you to the next destination.

" There is nothing more difficult
to take in hand, more perilous
to conduct, or more uncertain
in its success, than to take the
lead in the introduction of a
new order of things. "

—Niccolò Machiavelli

12

Inclusive Leadership

Effective change management ultimately depends on strong leadership. The leaders who struggle to get their people on board with a change versus those who are able to create buy-in and navigate change successfully tend to take different approaches.

Through my research into change management and personality, an effective model of leadership began to emerge—I call it inclusive leadership.

> ***Inclusive leadership:*** *The observable commitment to create workplaces that empower and lead team members to feel heard, recognized, valued, and appreciated by understanding the diverse perspectives of others.*

Inclusive leadership is a dynamic approach that actively involves all team members in the decision-making process and creates an environment where diverse thoughts are encouraged. This leadership strategy is especially valuable during change initiatives because it allows space for people to process change and invites them to become champions of change by including them in the initiative.

What does inclusive leadership look like in practice? There are eight competencies that define an inclusive leader. Evaluate your own leadership using the statements in the competencies list that follows—to what extent do you identify with these statements, and how do you practice them?

EIGHT COMPETENCIES OF INCLUSIVE LEADERSHIP

1. Empathy

- ☐ I seek to empathize with others and ensure they feel heard and understood.

- ☐ I anticipate the needs of others.

- ☐ I demonstrate sensitivity to others' feelings, goals, and needs through generous listening.

2. Curiosity

- ☐ I love to think up new ways of doing things.

- ☐ I prioritize learning more about the uniqueness of those I work with.

- ☐ I show an interest in exploring the uniqueness of those I work with.

3. Courage

- ☐ When I see an injustice happening to someone else, I speak up.

- ☐ I see mistakes as opportunities for myself and others to learn and grow.

- ☐ I openly share my awareness of my personal blind spots and biases.

4. Flexibility

- ☐ I thrive on change.

- ☐ I can vary my approach with ease based on the situation.

- ☐ I regularly seek out the perspectives of others, including those I lead.

5. Openness

- ☐ I make sure I manage and share my biases with others.

- ☐ I am willing to admit my mistakes.

- ☐ I believe there are many sides to most issues.

6. Tolerance

- ☐ I show commitment to create a space for diversity of thinking and making others feel included.

- ☐ I use and value diversity of thought to leverage the best possible outcome.

- ☐ I make other people feel welcome by being open-minded.

7. Leveraging Differences

- ☐ I can build rapport and trust easily with others who are different from me.

- ☐ I can see how my experiences and background are different from others.

- ☐ I am interested in people from different backgrounds and seek to include them.

8. Self-Awareness

- ☐ I accept responsibility for my actions, emotions, and behaviors.

- ☐ I know my strengths, personal qualities, blind spots, and biases.

- ☐ I show commitment to helping my team collaborate effectively and be inclusive of others.

These competencies are valuable for leaders at every level of an organization to display and are especially important during times of change.

Leadership is a skill that can be developed, and while most of these traits are influenced by behavioral style, personality, and upbringing, simply being conscious of your own strengths and weaknesses as an inclusive leader can help you become a stronger leader.

Perhaps the most important competency is empathy, which I believe should be a large focus during change efforts. Korn Ferry, a leading organizational management firm, describes empathy as the competency of the 21st century that leaders must leverage. It's a skill set that is very hard to develop if one does not harness empathy naturally.

How can people develop empathy?

- Be curious about others' lived experiences. Ask yourself what emotions you might be feeling if you were someone else. Think about the type of support they might want from you. Some people are disinclined to admit to needing support at all, so it's often better to think of specific actions you can take and ask whether those actions would be helpful.

- Use questions to better understand the person you're speaking with rather than making assumptions. Asking thoughtful questions can signal to the other person that you are curious about them or what they are feeling. Be careful not to barrage someone with questions as this might feel challenging.

- Listen. Focus entirely on what someone is telling you. Don't think about your response. Don't use your electronics. Engage fully with the human facing you and think about what they're saying and how they're feeling.

- Experience the world with a learning mindset to understand the diverse stories of others. Volunteer at an animal shelter, homeless shelter, or nursing home to get involved and learn from experience. Empathy is gained or strengthened from one's lived experiences.

Empathy is at the core of good leadership and serves as a guiding force through challenges and changes. It's a necessary component in order to establish trust and psychological safety within your team.

PSYCHOLOGICAL SAFETY

Teams and individuals need a sense of psychological safety in order to feel that they can speak their minds rather than just saying what they think the leader wants to hear. This is vital in a variety of leadership roles, from conducting one-on-one conversations to gauging the feelings of your team and understanding their challenges.

Psychological safety is perceived individually. Do they feel they can express themselves without fear of negative consequences to their image, status, or career? This can vary quite a bit from person to person, but take for example someone who is gay—do they feel comfortable talking about their partner at work? If someone has a lot of tattoos, do they have to cover them up because it's not considered professional?

There are five key ingredients to creating psychological safety:

1. Be approachable

2. Let your team make mistakes

3. Let your team propose new ideas

4. Be willing to discuss problems and find solutions

5. Care for your team

As a leader, you should be able to offer all of these ingredients all of the time.

It takes time to develop a sense of psychological safety in your team—it doesn't happen overnight. It's ultimately about building trust, which means you have to consistently demonstrate these traits. Ideally, leaders should strive toward creating psychological safety every day, not just when a change is happening or is about to happen.

A strong sense of psychological safety helps people navigate the change curve more quickly. In the acclimation phase, they need the freedom to make mistakes, propose ideas, and discuss problems and solutions. Without psychological safety, leaders will remain in the dark as their teams don't come forward with problems or ideas. In a worst-case scenario, that can lead to mismanaged or even failed change.

The term "psychological safety" was popularized by Amy Edmondson, author of the book *Psychological Safety*. In her book, she shares an example of nurses working with doctors where the nurses realized a need of the patient and would communicate that need to the doctor. The doctor would dismiss them and admonish them for questioning his recommendation. After being shut down by the doctor time and time again, at some point the nurses stopped communicating with the doctor.

In any type of business, if people aren't heard by their leaders, or if they're admonished or shut down, they're likely to stay silent next time. Important items will get swept under the carpet and overlooked without psychological safety.

I worked with an organization that had a leader who wanted things done in a very particular way. As a result, there was a lack of trust because no one could tell her, "I've fallen behind and can't make the deadline," or "I'm in over my head. I don't understand what you're saying." Instead, they just stayed quiet. As a result, problems lingered and worsened.

Psychological safety is key to a high-performing team because it is foundational to creating a positive work environment. Everyone has a limited amount of time and effort they can give to anything in a day. We often refer to time or income as discretionary, but people also have a limited amount of discretionary effort.

You get to decide what you spend your discretionary effort on, whether that's the company you work for or the leader you will go above and beyond for.

Where you decide to spend your discretionary effort depends a great deal on what matters to you, how much you trust your leader or your workplace, and how engaged you are with your job overall. If a change is draining a lot of the effort you have because you're emotionally exhausted or being asked to do a lot more than you were previously, you have less discretionary effort to spend.

When someone becomes disengaged from their role because they're unhappy with something, they're going to do what they need to do and nothing more. It's what many in human resources call a "quit and stay."

A team member who gives a lot of discretionary effort, doing more than what's needed, required, or requested of them, is a beautiful thing to have, and leaders shouldn't undervalue it. There's nothing a leader can do to *make* someone do that—people just do it because they like you or they like their job.

How do you build that motivation? Through inclusive leadership that creates a healthy, safe, and encouraging work environment.

FIVE BASES OF POWER

Holding a position of leadership comes with the responsibility of wielding power over other people, and there are a number of ways that can take shape. Excellent leaders recognize the power they hold and understand how to use the right type of power for their situation, while the worst leaders often choose the wrong type of power to reach the results they want to achieve.

The five bases of power were coined by psychologists John French and Bertram Raven in 1959. This model has certainly stood the test of time and leaders can be categorized by their uses of power.

The type of power someone wields is also affected by how people view the leader, displayed through certain behaviors. The different bases of power are core to leadership beyond just how you exert power. Understanding types of power allows you to be conscious of how they're affecting interactions within the workplace.

1. COERCIVE POWER

Coercive power is when a person of authority forces someone to comply with their request though a threat or punishment. It's sometimes paired hand in hand with reward power: If you comply, something good will happen; if you don't, something bad will happen.

Coercive power is not how leaders gain commitment, trust, loyalty, or followers when it comes to change. Leaders who take this approach may say, "Do as I say, period. That's just how it goes, and if you don't like it, there's the door."

Coercive power might work well in a situation such as a prison, but it is not appropriate in most work environments.

2. LEGITIMATE POWER

Legitimate power is given by someone in a leadership role to another person, and that position grants them power within the organization. Managers tend to have legitimate power that's given to them by the organization and recognized by the people they lead as a result of their position.

3. REWARD POWER

Reward power comes from the ability to offer someone a reward in exchange for compliance, such as monetary compensation or even intangible benefits such as praise. Reward power can be useful in change management, but it is also limited.

4. REFERENT POWER

Referent power relies on trust and respect and comes from a person's desire to be like others. It's about what other people think of the leader. A charismatic leader relies on referent power. Referent power can be extremely effective in enacting change, but it can be difficult to gain this kind of power in the first place.

5. EXPERT POWER

Expert power comes from a perception of the individual as skilled in their arena. A great example would be a doctor, who you listen to because you see them as an expert and trust them to give you good advice.

These types of power can be used not just by leaders but by anyone, and a champion of change who is viewed as an expert or has referent power from their team can be helpful in getting others to follow along with a change.

THOMAS-KILMANN CONFLICT MODEL

Similarly to understanding the different bases of power, it's also useful for leaders to understand how to approach conflict. Unfortunately conflict is often inherent in change, and effective change management often requires conflict management. It's like a two-sided coin: change on one side of the coin and conflict on the reverse.

One of my favorite tools for navigating conflict is the Thomas-Kilmann Instrument, also known as the TKI Conflict Mode Instrument. The instrument describes five modes of conflict. There isn't a single best mode to use—instead, people should choose their mode based on the situation.

These five modes can be viewed through two axes: assertiveness and cooperativeness. Assertiveness measures how someone goes about trying to satisfy their own concerns, while cooperativeness measures how one attempts to satisfy someone else's concerns.

These are the five modes of conflict in the TKI instrument:

- **Competing:** This power mode is assertive and uncooperative. The individual pursues their own needs or concerns at the expense of someone else.

- **Collaborating:** This mode seeks to find a solution that completely satisfies both people in a conflict. Each party digs into the issue to identify the other's underlying concerns.

- **Compromising:** This mode is about trying to find a quick middle ground, and it falls between competing and accommodating. It is both assertive and cooperative.

- **Avoiding:** This mode might be seen as a diplomatic way to sidestep or remove oneself from a threatening situation. It is unassertive and uncooperative, and it does not address the individual's needs or concerns nor the needs or concerns of the other person.

- **Accommodating:** This mode is the opposite of competing, where a person lets their needs or concerns go unmet in order to satisfy the needs or concerns of the other person. It is unassertive and cooperative and could be viewed as being selfless or submitting to someone else's point of view.

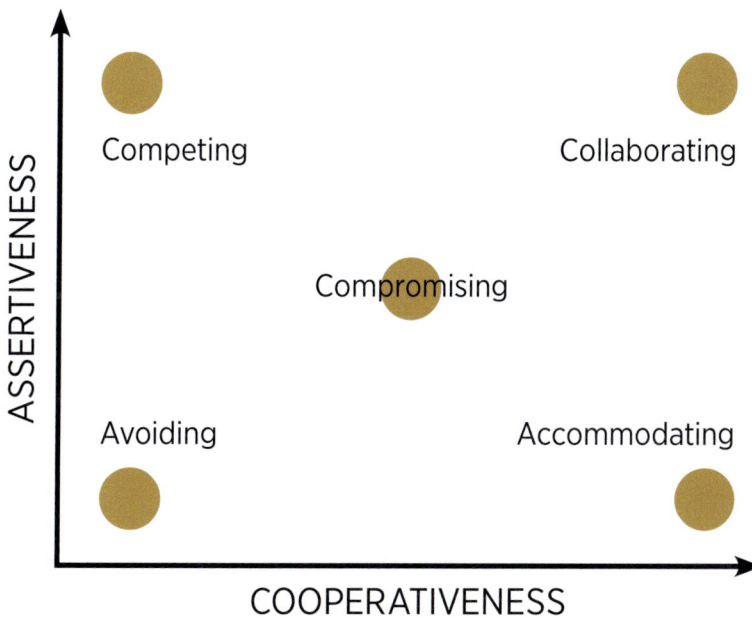

Competing   Collaborating

Compromising

Avoiding   Accommodating

ASSERTIVENESS

COOPERATIVENESS

(Copyright © 2009–2025 by Kilmann Diagnostics LLC. All rights reserved. Original figure is available at https://kilmanndiagnostics.com/overview-thomas-kilmann-conflict-mode-instrument-tki/)

Simply understanding the different approaches that are available to address conflict can be helpful to both leaders and their teams in choosing the best mode to use in a particular scenario. Certain modes of conflict are naturally easier than others depending on personality and other factors, so just like DISC behavioral styles, recognizing those tendencies in ourselves and others allows us to respond more thoughtfully.

HUMAN AGENCY

Inclusive leadership is built on human agency. By acknowledging and making space for the agency of others, you can lead much more effectively and empower your people to make positive choices.

When I'm coaching an executive, I never give advice. Advice is saved for consulting. Instead, I try to ask thoughtful questions to get people to come to a conclusion or decision from their own perspective. In general, people have the answers they need deep within themselves, and the art of a coach's role is to extract those answers.

When someone can come up with an idea or strategy themselves, they take more ownership of their task.

When someone understands what they do that contributes to the greater good or the purpose of the change, then they can develop a strategy to accomplish the new vision.

I worked with a family-owned business of less than 20 people that asked me to consult for them to evaluate how they could create new efficiencies. The operations manager had been doing her job for a long time but didn't come from an operations background— she'd been put in the role because she was related to the family. She wasn't performing at the level of her official title, or completing the role of an operations manager. I suggested that the owner

change her title to represent what she was actually doing or train her up to be an operations manager.

I created a report of all the things an operations manager should be doing and what she was and wasn't taking care of. I had a conversation with the owner first and then with the operations manager and asked her what kind of support or training she needed to reach the point where she could complete all the tasks and goals that were required of her. I framed it as just an opportunity for her and me to brainstorm.

People need to understand what the goal is if you're asking them to do something different.

You start by outlining the current state and the desired state, then identify what's missing. What's needed to fill the gap? How can you cross that chasm?

During a change, there is always a goal or vision and a gap between where the organization is now and where it needs to go, and every individual stakeholder will have to cross that chasm in one way or another. It's often more effective if an individual determines the steps they need to take to get from one state to another. And if they need to course-correct, they must make the decision on how to do so themselves.

There are four modes of human agency:

1. **Intentionality** – A personalized, self-determined strategy created to meet one's specific goals. (Intentionality can also be collective when the individual needs to involve others to create the plan.)

2. **Forethought** – The visualization of a future state needed to create the plan.

3. **Self-reactiveness** – The deliberate actions taken to reach the desired future state.

4. **Self-reflectiveness** – The ability to be self-aware and make corrections when given new information in order to course-correct if necessary.

If you give people the basic agency over their own roles to do what's needed to get where they need to go, they're more likely to succeed in getting there.

"Yesterday I was clever, so I wanted to change the world. Today I am wise, so I am changing **myself**."

—Jalaluddin Mevlana Rumi

13

Creating Change Through Learning

When companies undergo large changes, that requires people to learn to do things differently.

If people are expected to make a change, they will want to know *why*, *what*, and *how*. What they want to know first likely depends on their behavioral style—a C or S style likely wants to know the details of the *what* so they understand what they're required to do, while the D and I styles likely want to know the *why* first.

Generally, it's best to start with *why*, because it sets people up to learn.

Deutero learning is a term that comes from the Greek word *deuteron*, which means second, next, or farther from, and it refers to the idea of learning to learn. Learning can happen on multiple

levels and becomes deeper as someone iterates and takes in additional information to affect change.

Learning loops describe the cycle of learning, from taking in new information to applying it and reflecting on the process. A learning loop is a continuous cycle of learning and development that helps people retain knowledge and improve their understanding, from taking in new information to application and reflection.

Single loop learning is the simplest form of learning, like a single-lane highway. In this first level of learning, people ask the question, "Are we doing things right?" The answer is yes or no, and the aim is to figure out how to make a process better. It doesn't incorporate any change to company culture or strategy. Instead, it's simply about gathering information, and it's a necessary step to reach the next levels of learning.

Double loop learning takes learning a step further by asking, "Are we doing the right things?" This loop is about facilitating the process of change and helping others get through a change. You can think of it like an on-ramp merging into another lane, getting more complex than single-loop learning by taking in new information. Double-loop learning is self-reflective, allowing you to take in information and consider a different way of doing something, a new context, or a new perspective. Double-loop learning contains the possibility for transformation, and it is particularly important when a change is not effective because it allows you to examine what's going on and figure out the root of the problem.

Triple loop asks the question, "Is the decision-maker being virtuous or ethical?" Triple loop learning is key to transformation. If there's an acquisition, a change in leadership, or an initiative to change the company culture, triple-loop learning is necessary because it opens more questions to identify what needs to be done differently. Implementing change based on the first two learning loops requires getting buy-in during the triple loop stage, which is especially important at the highest levels of leadership in order to create effective change.

Single-loop learning typically doesn't require new information—it's simply a yes or no question about what's going on. Double-loop learning, which asks, "Are we doing the right things?" requires gathering new information and may involve some decision-making to determine what specifically needs to change and how something can be improved. Triple-loop learning evaluates what that says about your values and how you might move forward in the future.

Learning loops are a method for challenging rules, culture, and ways of working. If something isn't right, someone needs to be in charge of driving change. Each loop of learning reflects on the same question or topic in more depth, which will inform a wider range of decisions as well as the motivations for those decisions.

The reach of the learning also expands with each loop, from a single individual to an entire organization. The first loop can start with a single individual answering the yes or no question, but the second loop usually needs to bring in more people to get input, brainstorm possibilities, and gain more information. Finally, the third loop brings everyone involved into the process by creating buy-in. That process can start with a single individual at any level, depending on the scope of the change, whether that's someone in a single department or an upper-level executive bringing change to the organization as a whole.

Learning and change go hand in hand, and facilitating learning at every level of the organization is part of a strong change management strategy. Learning equips individuals with the knowledge and skills needed to adapt to new circumstances.

By understanding the underlying reasons for change and engaging in continuous learning through single, double, and triple loop processes, you can develop a culture of innovation, improvement, and ethical decision-making. This iterative process enhances both individual and collective growth, which helps facilitate successful implementation of change initiatives, ultimately leading to a more resilient and adaptive organization.

"It doesn't matter how strong your opinions are. If you don't use your power for positive change, you are indeed part of the problem."

—Coretta Scott King

14

Championing Change for Your Organization

Change is best facilitated through preparation that takes the psychology of individual responses into account. Ultimately, it's about enabling better communication among everyone involved. There are a variety of assessments that can be helpful in understanding behavioral styles and personalities so leaders can better prepare their teams for change.

I recommend starting with DISC assessments of all the change stakeholders to evaluate behavioral style. TTI Success Insights (TTI) offers an excellent assessment, and others are available as well. TTI also offers a motivators report, which describes 12 motivators from six domains, and it can be helpful in better understanding how different individuals function and respond to change.

What's important to keep in mind with interpreting DISC styles is that people usually have one or two styles that stand out clearly, but those styles don't define all of their actions. Instead, it's a matter of how much effort it takes to adapt to other styles. This is important because while certain people are sometimes better suited to certain things based on their behavioral style, that doesn't mean decisions should be made based on someone's DISC style. Knowing your style and tendencies can actually allow you to adapt more easily to other styles because it creates awareness of the factors at play.

When you administer an assessment, you need to decide how you want to use that information.

One goal might be to hold a workshop and have a team debrief their results together, or you may hire an external facilitator or consultant to debrief the assessments with the team, or you may have an internal HR person or external coach who can meet with individuals one-on-one to debrief their DISC results.

However you chose, understand that people may not feel comfortable opening up about their results to managers or HR personnel out of worry it might be used against them. They may feel they're being graded. Make a point to remind people that these conversations are for their personal and professional development and not to manage performance.

After conducting an assessment, it is valuable to conduct at least a short program to educate people about change and DISC. This helps people put their own behavioral style into perspective and creates awareness about how they and others navigate change. Education on topics such as the change curve, supporting others, and leading through change gives the team tools to help the change initiative succeed.

CHANGE WORKSHOPS

The purpose of a change workshop is to enable participants with a common language and understanding to better navigate change, and to make a business case for change to help people accept and commit to the initiative. The people receiving the training need to understand the purpose of it in order to buy into it and apply it practically.

I tend to start change workshops with the business case so participants understand the necessity of the change and then try to help them understand how they might respond during change. We review DISC styles and how each style may navigate change. We cover the psychological effects of change, including the three stages of evolution and the change curve, and explore strategies to navigate those stages.

I like to include experiential activities in our workshops to keep people engaged. This also helps people reflect on changes they've encountered and how they responded in the past. Getting someone to reflect in this way is the first step in enabling them to choose their mindset toward change.

One of the first activities we do is to place people in pairs and ask them to talk about "What's your favorite holiday?" After a minute and a half, a facilitator will rudely interrupt and say, "No matter where you are, we want you to change something."

People sometimes ask, "What should we change?" We don't give any clarity intentionally. The answer is that it doesn't matter; they just need to change something. Inevitably, there's confusion, which is exactly what we're trying to simulate—during organizational change, sometimes there's just not enough information provided, and people don't know what they're doing.

Acknowledgments

Thanks to my most memorable and supportive manager, Dennis Alderson. You allowed me to thrive and supported my dream of starting my own company.

To Target Training International (TTI) and Dr. Ron Bonnstetter, thank you for your invaluable insights, resources, and guidance during my research on change and DISC.

Most importantly, I'd like to thank my husband, Howard, who is my best cheerleader and supporter as we do life together.

And thanks to the team at Aloha Publishing, including Maryanna Young, Megan Terry, Rachel Langaker, and Heather Goetter, for their help in realizing my vision for this book and bringing it to the hands of readers.

We let them continue talking for another minute and a half and then interrupt and ask, "When we asked you to change something, how did you decide what to do differently?" Usually one person took initiative and did something, like took off their jacket, changed positions, or started talking about a different topic, and the other person followed along.

Another simple yet profound reflection prompt is to have people reflect on a recent major change they underwent. This invites people to think about how they didn't have enough information and how that affected their response. Maybe they were shocked, it happened at the last minute, and they had to go in to work the next day and act like everything was great. If they had any negative feedback about the change, they'd be viewed as a blocker, so they were afraid to ask questions even though they needed more information.

Workshops are beneficial for both leaders and their teams and can be customized to meet the needs of team members, departments, or the organization. A workshop can be done for just the highest level of leaders or for managers and then be rolled out to different departments or teams. Improving change management has to begin by educating leaders and expands from there.

If you'd like help in conducting a change workshop, you can find a host of support material including a facilitation kit and guide through Cooper Consulting Group at CooperConsultingGroup.com. You can also download the worksheets included in this book through the same website.

PREPARE YOUR TEAM FOR CHANGE

Educational programs about change are valuable for everyone, and it's best to conduct them before a large change is implemented so people have time to learn and process when they're not under additional stress.

Preparing for change and allowing enough time to process and manage the change effectively is one of the most important factors in its success.

Of course, it's not always feasible to adequately prepare your team for change in advance. Organizations need the agility to continuously respond to developments in their industry or the wider world. In that case, people are often learning how to manage change in the midst of the chaos.

During such a situation, it's especially important for leaders to provide support to their people. Everyone has to go through a period of reorientation, and it's okay for them to feel confused. It can be helpful to give them a framework or timeline of various milestones that need to be accomplished and ask for ideas about how they'd like to achieve those milestones. Let people try something using their own approaches. Check in on how they're doing personally. Clearly communicate roles and expectations for every person involved, no matter how low or high they are in the hierarchy.

Change is a psychological process, and it's necessary for people to go through the stages of evolution in order to come out on the other side and accept the change. Everybody goes through that process at a different speed. Some people might be more resilient than others, and those who accept the change quickly and have a positive view toward it can become your champions of change.

Each person handles change differently, and understanding how your colleagues process change helps you support them to get through the change.

About the Author

Christie is the founder and president of Cooper Consulting Group, and her mission is to inspire learning and leadership development to help leaders and teams perform at their best. Christie designs and facilitates customized workshops for individuals and leadership teams. She uses a portfolio of assessment and training tools to identify root causes of workplace challenges, enhance communication, and build effective leadership.

Before founding Cooper Consulting Group, Christie built a successful career in the corporate world, holding senior leadership roles as a regional manager and corporate trainer with Mars, Inc., which provided her a practical understanding of the challenges leaders face. Today, she brings that real-world perspective into every client engagement, helping organizations bridge the gap between strategy and execution.

Christie's academic achievements reflect her commitment to leadership excellence. She holds both a Ph.D. in global leadership and change from Pepperdine University and an Ed.D. in organizational leadership. A lifelong learner, she has earned credentials as a master MBTI® practitioner, board-certified coach, certified trainer in emotional intelligence, and certified analyst in behaviors and motivators.

Christie's unique blend of academic expertise, corporate leadership, and consulting practice makes her a trusted resource for leaders and future professionals alike.

Connect

If you would like to connect with the author,
reach out to Cooper Consulting Group.

CooperConsultingGroup.com

Resources

To purchase my Change Facilitation Kit,
the TKI Interpretive Report, or the DISC assessment,
go to www.AssessmentsForSuccess.com

For more on programs mentioned in the book, go to

CooperConsultingGroup.com/GuidingChange
CooperConsultingGroup.com/ManagingConflict
CooperConsultingGroup.com/InclusiveLeadership
CooperConsultingGroup.com/Disc-Workshops

Endnotes

IPIP. 2019. "International Personality Item Pool" https://ipip.ori.org/

Kilmann Diagnostics. 2019. "An Overview of the Thomas-Kilmann Conflict Mode Instrument (TKI) a Long-Term Collaboration by Kenneth W. Thomas and Ralph H. Kilmann - Kilmann Diagnostics." https://kilmanndiagnostics.com/overview-thomas-kilmann-conflict-mode-instrument-tki/

Kempton, Lisa. 2021. "Managing Resistance to Change Overview." Prosci.com. March 30, 2021. https://www.prosci.com/managing-change-resistance

Statista, 2024. "Number of M&A Deals in the U.S. 2000-2020." https://www.statista.com/statistics/914665/number-of-ma-deals-usa/

Praise for

GUIDING CHANGE

"Dr. Cooper's new book, *Guiding Change,* is the most comprehensive discussion of the change process that I have ever encountered. She masterfully presents the essence of managing change for organizations and their members—with the most practical action recommendations that transform good intentions into effective results at every step along the way. Given the accelerating pace of change in today's world, I highly recommend this book for everyone who wishes to improve how they manage and cope with incessant organizational change."

—Ralph H. Kilmann, Ph.D., CEO of Kilmann Diagnostics and co-author of the Thomas-Kilmann Conflict Mode Instrument (TKI)

"*Guiding Change* brilliantly captures a truth hidden in plain sight—the ability to drive change is *the* work of today's leaders preparing their organizations to adapt to and succeed in today's hyper competitive world."

—Mark D. Cohen, J.D., former Department of Defense leader and author of *The Young Leader*

"Christie Cooper has drawn from her executive experience and exceptional academic background to create a leadership narrative that is both rich in substance and easy to read. It doesn't belong on a bookshelf, but on a desk where leaders can pick it up regularly to reflect on their own relationships and performance."

—Phil Hansen, Chief of Police (retired) and Director Emeritus, National Tactical Officer's Association

"It's an honor to acknowledge the meaningful contribution *Guiding Change* by Christie Cooper brings to the conversation around leadership and change. Managing change is one of the most challenging aspects of leadership, yet Christie approaches it with a rare combination of academic insight and real-world experience that makes the topic feel both approachable and empowering.

"By tapping into the power of DISC assessments and exploring how personality impacts our response to change, she offers an innovative, actionable framework that leaders can truly use. What makes this book stand out is Christie's ability to blend her research with relatable stories from the field, creating a resource that's as engaging as it is useful.

"*Guiding Change* isn't just another book on theoretical change management; it's a practical, insightful resource for navigating it with intention and confidence. I highly recommend it as a powerful tool to enhance communication, strengthen team connections, and elevate your leadership through times of change."

—Ingrid Middleton-Mahar, Vice President of People and Culture, Blackrock Holdings

"Reading *Guiding Change* feels like sitting down with a wise advisor who's been through it all. It's approachable and full of strategies you can use right away."

—Shomari White, Chief Operating Officer, The George Washington University

"*Guiding Change* breaks down the tools and knowledge that Christie Cooper has shared in her workshops with our team. These skills truly helped guide our leadership through two major changes in the past, flattening our leadership structure and acquiring a second manufacturing site. You can't make someone change. You can only create an environment that inspires or motivates people to do something."

—Douglas McIntyre, President of Weber Metals, Inc.

"As a retired senior executive in federal law enforcement, *Guiding Change* by Christie Cooper struck a deep chord with me. Leading change in our world isn't theoretical—it's personal, urgent, and at times painful. We deal with people's careers, their sense of purpose, and sometimes their very identity. Christie Cooper gets that. Her book is more than a guide—it's a lifeline for leaders who must drive transformation while holding the line on integrity, trust, and morale. Her approach, grounded in behavioral science and real-world experience, gave voice to what many of us feel but struggle to articulate: change isn't just strategy—it's deeply human. The DISC framework she applies is a powerful lens for understanding those we lead and how to bring them with us through the storm. Every leader in federal service should read this book—it's that important."

—John D. Masters, MBA, Ph.D. (ABD), Retired Senior Executive Federal Law Enforcement Officer

"*Guiding Change* is a fantastic blueprint on how to understand and respect individuals navigating through change. As a VP of a Fortune 300 company, now turned entrepreneur, I can attest that this guide is not only valuable but essential for business leaders today and in the years to come. We've all witnessed enterprise-wide investments fail because of resistance to change. With this new book, Dr. Cooper has given us solutions to ensure a more human-centered approach to change and, ultimately, transformation."

—Sanchia Patrick, Principal, Be & Why, LLC

"Dr. Cooper takes us through ways to not only make changes in our own lives and leadership styles, but more importantly shows us how to inspire change in others: change that will last and make a positive difference. We all know the phrase 'the only constant is change.' She teaches us how to make positive changes that will stick and that will make things better for ourselves, our teams, and our customers. Grab this book and invest the next two hours in yourself and the people you lead."

—Ed Hart, CEO of Hart Leadership Group and Host of *From the Hart Podcast*